POWER OF MASTERY OF SELF

OR POISE

D. STARKE

POWER OF MASTERY OF SELF OR POISE

For information and contact visit our website at:
IndoEuropeanPublishing.com

The present edition is a revised version of 1916 of this work published by Funk & Wagnalls, NY, under the title: *Poise: How to Attain It*, produced in the current edition with completely new, easy to read format, and is set and proofread by Alfred Aghajanian for Indo-European Publishing.

Cover Design by Indo-European Design Team

ISNB: 978-1-60444-048-5

IndoEuropean
Publishing.com
Los Angeles, CA, USA

PREFACE

All efforts directed toward the correcting of temperamental or mental blemishes or defects and nervous conditions are of benefit to humanity. In producing this book the Author's purpose was to help the readers to overcome these weaknesses, which are a serious impediment to mental development, and hinder personal advancement and general progress. The aim of the Publishers in issuing this translation is to put into the hands of those who wish to overcome their failings, become masters of themselves, and command the attention and respect of others, a work that has been thoroughly tested abroad and one that will be found of exceptional service in attaining the end in view—the securing of a perfect balance.

This book is written in two parts. The first points to the need of Poise in daily life, indicates the obstacles to be overcome, and discusses the effects of Poise on personal efficiency. The second instructs the reader how to secure that evenness of temperament which is the chief characteristic of Poise. It includes, in addition, a series of practical physical exercises to be used in acquiring Poise.

If such a work as this is to do good, if the reader really wishes to benefit by the advice that it gives him, it must be read thoughtfully and diligently, not fitfully and forgetfully, and the reader most steadfastly keep before him the maxim of the Author—"Poise is a power derived from the Mastery of Self."

THE PUBLISHERS

CONTENTS

PART I

POISE: ITS NEED, ITS ENEMIES, ITS EFFECT

CHAPTER I

THE NEED OF POISE IN LIFE

Lack of poise has always been an obstacle to those who are imbued with the desire to succeed.

In every age the awkwardness born of timidity has served to keep back those who suffered from it, but this defect has never been so great a drawback as in the life of today.

The celebrated phrase of the ancient Roman writer who said, "Fortune smiles on the brave," could very well serve as our motto nowadays, with this slight alteration: "Fortune smiles on those who are possessed of poise."

At this point let us attempt an exact definition of poise.

It is a quality which enables us to judge of our own value, and which, in revealing to us the knowledge of the things of which we are really capable, gives us at the same time the desire to accomplish them.

It is not a quality wholly simple. On the contrary, it is a composite of many others all of which take part in the molding of that totality which bears the name of poise.

It may be well to pass in review the principal qualities of which it is composed, that one may characterize as follows:

Will.

Reason.

Knowledge of one's own value.

Correctness of judgment.

Sincerity toward oneself.

The power of resisting the appeals of self-love.

Contempt of adverse criticism.

Pride that is free from vanity.

A definite and clearly conceived ambition.

Will, as is well known, is the pivot of all our resolutions, whether the question for the moment be how to form them or how to keep them when formed.

A man without will-power is a straw, blown about by every wind and carried, whether he will or no, into situations in which he has no valid reason for finding himself.

Without the will-power which enables us to take a firm hold of ourselves and to get a grip on our impressions, they will remain vague and nebulous without presenting to us characters of sufficient definiteness to enable us to direct them readily into the proper channels.

It is will-power which gives us the force to maintain a resolution which will lead us to the hoped-for goal of success.

It is will-power also which enables us to correct the faults which stand in the way of the acquiring of poise.

We are not now speaking of those idle fancies which are no more than manifestations of nervousness. We have in mind rather that controlled and enduring purpose which arms the heart against the assaults of the emotions by giving it the strength to overcome them.

There are many cases even in which will-power has led to their entire suppression.

This happens more particularly in the case of those artificial emotions that the man of resolution ignores completely, but which cause agony to the timid who do not know how to escape them, and exaggerate them to excess.

This abnormal development of their personalities is the peculiarity of the timid, which their fitful efforts of will only heighten, alienating from them the sympathy which might be of assistance to them.

They take refuge in a species of mischievous and fruitless activity, leaving the field open to the development of all sorts of imaginary ills that argument does not serve to combat.

Their ego, whose importance is in no way counterbalanced by their appreciation of the friends they keep at a distance, fills their entire existence to such an extent that they have no doubt whatever that, when they are in public, every eye is, of necessity, fixed on them.

Their negative will leaves them at the mercy of every sort of emotion, which, in arousing in them the necessity of a reaction they feel themselves powerless to realize, reduces them to a state of inferiority that, when it becomes known, is the source of grave embarrassment to them.

The power of will which sustains those who wish to acquire the habit of poise is, then, the capacity to accomplish acts solely because one has the ardent desire to achieve them.

We are now speaking, understand, neither of extreme heroism or of impossibilities.

Another point presents itself here. Willpower, in order to preserve its energy, must be sustained and fixed. At this price alone can we achieve poise. We must, therefore, thoroughly saturate ourselves with this principle: Reasoning-power is an essential element in the up-building of poise.

It is reasoning-power which teaches us to distinguish between those things that we must be careful to avoid and those which are part and parcel of the domain of exaggeration and fantasy.

It is also by means of reasoning that we arrive at the proper appreciation of the just mean that we must observe. It is by its aid that we are enabled to disentangle those impulses that will prove profitable from a chaos of useless risks.

It is always by virtue of deductions depending on reason that we are able to adopt a resolution or to maintain an attitude that we believe to be correct, while preserving our self-possession under circumstances in which persons of a timorous disposition would certainly lose their heads.

Those who know how to reason never expose themselves to the possibility of being unhorsed by fate for lack of good reasons for strengthening themselves in their chosen course.

They adhere, in the very heat of discussion and in spite of the onslaughts of destiny, to the line of conduct that sage reflection has taught them to adopt and are more than careful never to abandon it except for the most valid reasons.

They never stray into the byways in which the timid and the shrinking constantly wander without sufficient thought of the goal toward which they are journeying.

They know where they are going, and if, now and again, they ask for information about the road that remains to be traveled, it is with no intention of changing their course, but simply so as not to miss the short cuts and to lose nothing of the pleasures of the scenes through which they may pass.

Reasoning-power is the trade-mark of superior minds. Mediocre natures take no interest in it and, as we have seen, the timid are incapable of it, except in so far as it follows the beaten path.

True poise never is guided by anything but reason. Certain risks can never be undertaken save after ripe deliberation.

Confusion is never the fate of those who are resolved on a definite line of conduct.

Such people are careful to plumb the questions with which they have to grapple and to weigh the inconveniences and the advantages of the acts they have the desire to accomplish.

When their decision is once made, however, nothing will prevent the completion of the work they have begun. Such people are ripe for success.

The knowledge of one's real worth is a quality doubly precious when contrasted with the fact that the majority of people are more than indulgent to their own failings. Of many of them it may be said, in the words of the Arab proverb, couched in the language of imagery: "This man has no money, but in his pocket everything turns to gold."

This saying, divested of the language of hyperbole, means simply that the man in question is so obsessed with the greatness of his own personal value that he exaggerates the importance of everything that concerns him.

This condition is a much more common one than one might at first believe. Many an occurrence which, when it happens to some one else, seems to us quite devoid of interest, becomes, when it directly affects us, a matter to compel the attention of others, to the extent that we find ourselves chilled and disappointed when we discover that we are the victims of that indifference which we were prepared to exhibit toward other people under similar circumstances.

The consciousness of our own worth must not be confounded with that adoration of self which transforms poise into egotism.

It is a good thing to know one's own powers sufficiently well to undertake only such tasks as are certainly within the scope of one's abilities.

To believe oneself more capable than one really is, is a fault that is far too common. It is, nevertheless, less harmful in the long run than the failing which is its exact antithesis. Lack of confidence in one's own powers is the source of every kind of feebleness and of all unsuccess.

It is for this reason that poise never can exist without another quality, that correctness of judgment which, in giving us the breadth of mind to know exactly how much we are capable of, permits us to undertake our tasks without boasting and without hesitation.

Soundness of judgment is the faculty of being able to appreciate the merits of our neighbors without cherishing any illusions as to our own, and of being able to do this so exactly that we can with assurance carry out to its end any undertaking, knowing that the result must be, barring accidents, precisely what we have foreseen.

This being the case, what possible reason can we have for depreciating ourselves or for lacking poise?

Timid people suffer without recognizing their own

defects in the matter of insight.

They torture themselves by building their judgments on indications and not on facts.

If the perception of a man of resolution causes him to understand at once the emptiness of criticisms based on envy or spleen, the timid man, always ready to seize on anything that can be possibly construed into an appearance of ridicule directed against himself, will give up a project that he hears criticized without stopping to weigh the value of the arguments advanced.

Far from arguing the question out, or attempting a rebuttal, he never even dreams of it. The very thought of a contest, however courteously it may be conducted, frightening him to such an extent that he loses all his ideas.

The unfortunate shrinking which characterizes him makes him an easy prey for people of exaggerated enthusiasms as well as to quick disillusionment.

A token of apparent sympathy touches him so profoundly that he does not wait to estimate its value and to decide whether it be sincere or not.

He passes in a moment from careless gaiety to the blackest despair if he imagines that he has observed even the appearance of an unsympathetic gesture.

He does not need to be sure, to be miserable. It is enough for him if the circumstances that he thought favorable become seemingly hostile and antagonistic.

How utterly different is the attitude of the man who is endowed with poise!

His firmness of soul saves him from unconsidered enthusiasms and he jealously preserves his control in the presence of excessive protestations as well as when confronting indications of aimless antagonism.

How can such a man as this possibly fail to form a correct judgment and to benefit by all the qualities that depend on it?

Absolute sincerity toward oneself is one of the forms of sound judgment.

Without indulging in excessive modesty, it is a good thing to endeavor to become intimately acquainted with one's aptitudes and one's failings, and to admit the latter with the utmost frankness in order to set about the work of correcting them.

It is also necessary to know exactly what sort of territory it is in which one is taking one's risks.

The world of affairs, whatever these last may happen to be, may be likened to a vast preserve containing traps for wild beasts.

The man who wishes to walk in such a place without coming to harm will, first of all, make a careful study of the ground for the purpose of avoiding the traps and pitfalls that may engulf him or wound him as he passes.

Just as soon as he has located these dangers his step becomes firm and he can advance with a tranquil gait and head upraised along the paths which he knows do not conceal any dangerous surprises.

These are the pitfalls that most frequently threaten that daring that we sometimes find in the timid.

Their very defects preventing them from making proper comparisons, they are altogether too prone to ignore their faults and to magnify their virtues and so fall an easy prey to the designer and the sharper.

Their very carelessness in estimating other people becomes the foundation of an involuntary partiality the moment they are called on to judge their own actions.

It is not deliberate self-indulgence that drives them to act in this way, but their inexperience, which gives rise in them to the desire for perfection, and this necessarily provokes, simultaneously with the despair caused by their failure to attain it, a fear of having this failure remarked or commented on.

The man who possesses poise is too familiar with the realities of life not to be aware that the search for such an ideal is a Utopian dream.

But he is also aware that, if actual perfection does not exist, it is the bounden duty of man to struggle always in pursuit of good and to show appreciation of it in whatsoever form it may manifest itself.

Sincerity toward himself thus becomes for him an

easy matter indeed, and for the very reason that his poise leaves him absolutely free to form a correct estimate of others.

Serious self-examination throws a clear light for him on those merits of which he has a right to be proud, while revealing to him at the same time the faults to which he is most likely to yield.

The habit of estimating himself and his own qualities without fear or favor gives him great facility for gaging the motives of other people.

He thus avoids the pitfalls that a biased viewpoint spreads before the feet of the foolish, and at the same time represses that feeling of vanity which might lead him to believe that he is altogether too clever to fall into them.

He watches himself constantly to avoid getting into the bypaths which he sees with sorrow that others are following, and does not fail to estimate accurately the value of the victories he achieves over himself as well as over the duplicity of most of the people who surround him.

And this superiority is what makes certain his poise. More difficult perhaps than anything else to acquire is the power to resist the appeals of one's own self-love.

We will explain this later at greater length. Lack of poise is often due to nothing so much as an excess of vanity which throws one back on oneself from the fear of not being able to shine in the front rank.

Such a person does not say to himself: "I will

conquer this place by sheer merit." He contents himself with envying those who occupy it, quite neglecting to put forth the efforts which would place him there beside them.

There is nothing worse than yielding to an exaggerated tenderness toward ourselves, which, by magnifying our merits in our own eyes, frequently leads us to make attempts which result in failure and expose us to ridicule.

This is a most frequent cause of making an inveterate coward of one who is subject to occasional attacks of timidity.

To know one's limitations exactly and never to allow oneself to exceed them—this is the part of wisdom, the act of a man who, as the saying goes, knows what he is about.

There is in every effort a necessary limit that it is not wise to exceed.

"Never force your talents," says a very pithy proverb. Never undertake to do a thing that is beyond your powers.

Never allow yourself to be drawn into a discussion on a subject which is beyond your intellectual depth. To do so is to take the risk of making mistakes that will render you ridiculous.

But if you are quite convinced that you can come out victorious, never hesitate to enter a trial of wits that may serve as an occasion for demonstrating the fact that you are sure of your subject.

The man who cultivates poise will never let pass such opportunities as this for exhibiting himself in a favorable light.

Conscious of the soundness of his own judgment, and filled with a real sincerity toward himself, he will not allow himself to be carried away by a possible chance of success. Rather will he gather himself together, collect his forces, and wait until he can achieve a real effect on the minds of those whom he wishes to impress.

Similarly the result of not succeeding in such a venture is obvious. It has the effect of developing a distrust of oneself and of destroying the superb assurance of those people of whom it is often said: "Oh, he! He is sailing with the wind at his back!"

People generally fail to add in these cases that such persons have left nothing undone to accomplish this result and are more than careful not to weigh anchor when the wind is not favorable.

It is true enough that there can be no actual shelter from a storm, but the mariner who is prepared is able to ride it out without appreciable damage, while those who are not prepared generally founder on account of their poor seamanship.

Disregard of calumny is always the index of a noble spirit.

The man who wastes time over such indignities and who allows himself to be affected by them is not of the stature that insures victory in the struggle.

Minds of large caliber disdain these manifestations of futile jealousy.

People of obscurity are never vilified. Only those whose merits have placed them in the limelight are the targets for the attacks of envy and for the slanders of falsehood.

A precept that has often been enunciated, and can not be too often repeated, which should, indeed, be inscribed in letters of gold over the doors of every institution where men meet together, runs as follows: "Envy and malice are nothing more than homage rendered to superiority."

Only those who occupy an enviable position can become objects of calumny.

Such calumny is always the work of the unworthy, who think to advertise their own merits by denying those of better men.

Men of resolution under such circumstances simply shrug their shoulders and pass by.

The rest, those who are enslaved by timidity, become confused.

Their ego, which they cultivated in a fashion at once obscure and absolute, becomes so profoundly affected that they lack all courage to openly defend it.

Moreover, that instinctive need of sympathy, which is so marked a characteristic of the timid, is deeply wounded, while their chronic fear of disapprobation is strengthened by the criticisms spread abroad.

The illogicality of these sentiments is obvious. The man who is timid shuns society, yet nevertheless the judgments of this same society are for him a question of absorbing interest. Timidity is, in effect, a disease of many forms, every one of which is founded on illogicality.

It is always a mental weakness. It is sometimes vanity, but never pride, that reasonable pride that a philosophy now abandoned once numbered as one of the principal vices, and which, if rightly estimated, can be considered as the motive power of every noble action.

Pride is a force. It is therefore a virtue which must of necessity be one of the components of poise, so long as it contains within it no seeds of vanity. Under such circumstances it is a primal condition of success in the achievement of poise. Pride must, however, be free from vanity, otherwise it ceases to be a force and becomes a cause of deterioration.

As a matter of fact, those who are conceited are always the dupes of their own desire to bulk largely in the minds of others, and at the mere thought that they will not shine as they have hoped to do the majority of them are put entirely out of countenance and are quite at a loss for means of expression.

The inevitable result of this tendency is to drive them into association with mediocrity. In such a society alone will the vain find themselves at their ease. But the very moment that they find themselves in the presence of those who are their superiors, the fear of not being able to occupy the front rank throws them into such a state of mental disarray that they entirely lose their assurance and that appearance of poise by whose aid they are often able to deceive others.

Finally, one of the most solid elements of poise is, without doubt, a well-defined ambition, that is to say, one that is divested of the drawbacks of frivolity and directly winged toward the goal of one's hopes.

The man who possesses ambition of this kind is certainly destined to acquire, if he has not already acquired it, that poise which is absolutely necessary to him in order to make his way in the world.

He will neither be pretentious nor timorous, exaggerated nor fearful. He will go forward without hesitation toward the goal which he knows to be before him, and will make, without any apologies, those detours which seem to him necessary to the success of his undertaking, without paying any attention to the fruitless distractions that make victims of the rash.

He will not have to put up with the affront of being refused, for he will ask aid only of those persons who, for various reasons, he is practically sure will be of assistance to him. The knowledge of his own deserts, while keeping him in the position he has attained, will prevent him from being satisfied in commonplace surroundings, and his will-power will always maintain him at the level he has reached, permitting him no latitude save that of exceeding it.

Such is true poise, not that whose spirit one violates by merely associating it with the incapable, the pretentious, or the extravagant, but that which is at once the motive power and the inspiration of all the actions of those who, in their determination to force their way through the great modern struggle for existence, perseveringly follow a line of conduct that they have worked out for themselves in advance.

Ignoring such enterprises as they know to be unworthy of their powers, those who are possessed of real poise (and not of that foolish temerity colloquially known as *bluff*) will devote themselves solely to such tasks as a well-ordered judgment and an accurate knowledge of their own potentialities indicate to them to be fitting.

Does this mean that they will succeed in every case?

Unfortunately, no! But such of them as have met with temporary failure, if they are able to assure themselves that their lack of success has been due neither to a failure of will-power nor a fear of ridicule, will return to the charge, once more prepared to make headway against circumstances which they have the poise to foresee, and which they will at least render incapable of harming them, even if they lack the necessary force to dominate them completely to their own advantage.

CHAPTER II

THE ENEMIES OF POISE

The enemies of poise are many and of different origins, both of feeling and of impulse.

They all tend, however, toward the same result, the cessation of effort under pretexts more or less specious.

It is of no use deceiving ourselves. Lack of poise has its roots deep in all the faults which are caused by apathy and purposeless variety.

We have learned in the previous chapter how greatly the vice of lack of confidence in oneself can retard the development of the quality we are considering.

Balanced between the desire to succeed and the fear of failure, the timid man leads a miserable existence, tortured by unavailing regrets and by no less useless aspirations, which torment him like the worm that will never be quenched.

Little by little the habit of physical inaction engenders a moral inertia and the victim learns to fly from every opportunity of escaping from his bondage.

Very soon an habitual state of idleness takes possession of him and causes him to avoid everything that tends to make action necessary.

The dread of responsibility that might devolve on him turns him aside from every sort of endeavor, and he passes his life in a hopeless and sluggish inaction, from a fear of drawing down on himself reproaches to which he might have to make answer or of being compelled to take part in discussions which would involve the disturbing of his indolent repose.

Are we to suppose then that he finds real happiness in such a state of things?

Certainly not, for this negative existence weighs on him with all the burden of a monotony that he feels powerless to throw off. His own mediocrity enrages him while the success of others fills him with dismay.

Nevertheless his weakness of character allows the hate of action to speak more loudly to him than legitimate ambition, and keeps him in a state of obvious inferiority that of itself gives birth to numberless new enemies, who end by destroying him utterly.

He is first attacked by slowness of comprehension, the inevitable consequence of that idleness that causes the cowardly to shun the battle.

Rather than combat influences from without he allows them daily to assume a more prominent and a more definite place in his thoughts.

His hatred of action says no to all initiative and he considers that he has accomplished his whole duty toward society and toward himself when he says: "What's the use of undertaking this or that? I haven't a chance of succeeding and it is therefore idle to invite defeat!"

So quickly does the change work that his mind, from lack of proper exercise, rapidly reaches the condition where it can not voluntarily comprehend any but the most simple affairs and goes to pieces when confronted with occasions that call for reflection or reasoning, which he considers as the hardest kind of work.

It is hardly a matter for astonishment, therefore, that under these conditions effeminacy should take possession of a soul that has become the sport of all the weaknesses that are born of a desire to avoid exertion.

We do not care to draw the picture of that case too often encountered in which this moral defeat becomes changed into envy, the feeling of bitterness against all men, the veritable hell of the man who has not the power to make the effort that shall free him.

Mental instability is the inevitable consequence of this state of affairs.

All brain-activity being regarded as a useless toil, the man of timidity never understands the depth of the questions he has not the courage to discuss. If he does talk of them, it is with a bias rendered all the more prejudiced by the fact that, instead of expressing his ideas, he takes refuge in fortifying his heresies with arguments of which the smallest discussion would demonstrate the worthlessness.

This unwillingness to discuss conditions gives rise among people who are deficient in poise to a special form of reasoning, which causes them to summarize in the most hurried fashion even the gravest events, on the sole consideration that they are not asked to take part in them. If, by any chance, they are forced to be actors in these events the least little incident assumes for them the most formidable proportions.

It seems probable that this tendency to exaggerate everything with which they come in contact is due solely to egoism. It is certain at any rate that egoism plays a large part in it, but some portion of it is due to the lack of observation that characterizes all people of timidity.

The mental idleness and the instability of mind that we have already considered render such people less inclined to consider with any degree of care those things which do not touch them directly.

At this stage, it is no longer possible for them to feign ignorance in order to avoid the trouble of thinking, and they are only touched, even by the most personal matters, to the extent that circumstances impose on them the necessity of thinking or of acting with reference to the subject under consideration.

The idea that they can no longer avoid the resolutions which must be made and their fear of the consequences which may result from these affect them to such a profound extent that the most insignificant of occurrences immediately assumes for them an altogether incommensurate importance.

This state of mind is a notable foe of poise. It is practically impossible for a person under such conditions to believe that any considerable effort he has made can have passed unperceived.

This propensity to assign an exaggerated importance to personal affairs develops egoism, the avowed enemy of poise. An egoist necessarily assumes that the rest of the world attributes to his acts the importance he himself assigns to them.

This preoccupation does not fail to upset him. It increases his embarrassment and the fear of not appearing in the light in which he wishes to be seen paralyzes him, while the dread of what other people may think prevents him from being himself.

To this cause many otherwise inexplicable defeats must be assigned, the result of which is a renewed resentment against the world at large and an ardent desire to avoid any further exposure to the chance of failure.

A case in point is the man who becomes nervous while making a speech, starts to stammer, and makes a lamentable failure of what began well enough, because he imagines that persons in the audience are making fun of him.

He has overheard a word, or surprised a look, neither of which had any relation to him, but so great is his egoism that he does not dream that any one in the audience can be so lacking in taste as to be concerned with anything but himself.

Had this man, in spite of his egoism, been endowed with poise, he would have gone along calmly, simply forcing himself to ignore all criticism and to impress his very critics by his attitude and his eloquence. But his distrust of himself, his mental instability, his habitual weakness of reasoning, all these enemies of poise league themselves together to inflict on him a defeat, of which the memory will only aggravate his nervousness and his desire never to repeat such an unpleasant experience.

For the man who has no poise there is no snatching victory from defeat. His feeble will-power is completely routed, and the effort involved in stemming the tide of adverse opinion is to him an impossibility.

From dread of being carried away by the current, and feeling himself incapable of struggling against it, he prefers to hide himself in the caves along the shore, rather than to make one desperate effort to cross the stream.

But the very isolation he seeks, in depriving him of moral support, increases his embarrassment.

"It is not good for man to be alone," says Holy Writ. It is certainly deplorable, for one who desires to make his way, to find himself without a prop, without a counselor, and without a guide.

This is the case of those timid persons who do not understand how to make friends for themselves.

Poise, on the other hand, invites sympathy. It aids men to expand. It creates friends when needed, and weaves the bonds of comradeship and of protection without which our social fabric could not hold together.

Educators should seek for inspiration in the lessons that the exigencies of modern life offer to the view of the observer. Excessive modesty, sworn enemy of poise, is, socially speaking, a fault from which young minds should be carefully guarded.

It is the open door to all the feeblenesses which interfere with the development of poise.

It is a mistake that it has so long been considered as a virtue.

In any case, the day of extreme humility is past. This detachment from oneself is contrary to all the laws of progress.

It is opposed to all the principles of evolution and of growth which should be the study of all our contemporaries, whatever their station or the class to which they may happen to belong.

No man has the right to withdraw himself from the battle and to shirk his duties, while watching other people fighting to maintain the social equilibrium and seeking to achieve the position to which their talents and their attainments render them worthy to aspire.

That which is too easily honored with the title of modesty is generally nothing more than a screen behind which conscious ineptitude conceals itself.

It is a very easy thing to strike a disdainful attitude and to exclaim: "I didn't care to compete!"

Do not forget that a defeat after a sanguinary combat is infinitely more honorable than a retreat in which not a blow is struck.

Moreover, the combats of the mind temper the soul, just as those of the body fortify the flesh, by making both fit for the victory that is to be.

It is then against the enemies of poise that we must go forth to war.

Cowardice must be hunted down, wherever we encounter it, because its victims are thrown into the struggle of life burdened with an undeniable inferiority.

Even if they are worth while no one will be found to observe it, since their lack of poise always turns them back on themselves, and very few people have the wit to discover what is so sedulously concealed.

Deception is the necessary corollary of this, and one that very soon becomes changed into spite. The disappointment of being misunderstood must inevitably lead us to condemn those who do not comprehend us. Our shyness will be increased at this and we shall end by disbelieving ourselves in the qualities that we find other people ignoring in us.

From this condition of discouragement to that of mental inertia it is but a step, and many worthy people who lack poise have rapidly traveled this road to plunge themselves into the obscurity of renunciation.

They are like paralytics. Like these poor creatures they have limbs which are of no service to them and which from habitual lack of functioning end by becoming permanently useless.

If their nature is a bad one they will have still more reason to complain of this lack of poise, with its train of inconveniences of which we have been treating, that will leave them weakened and a prey to all sorts of mental excesses which will be the more serious in their effects for the fact that their existence is known to no one but the victims.

Instead of admitting that their lack of poise-due to the various faults of character we have been discussing—is the sole cause of the apparent ostracism from which they suffer, they indulge in accusations against fate, against the world, against circumstances, and grow to hate all those who have succeeded, without being willing to acknowledge that they have never seriously made the attempt themselves.

Only those return home with the spoils who have taken part in the battle, have paid with their blood and risked their lives.

The man who remains in hiding behind the walls of his house can hardly be astonished that such honors do not come his way.

Life is a battle, and victory is always to the strong. The timid are never called on to take their share of the booty. It becomes the property of those who have had the force to win it, either by sheer courage or by cautious strategy, for real bravery is not always that which calls for the easy applause of the crowd.

It is found just as much among those who have the will-power to keep silent as to their plans and to resist the temptation to actions which, while satisfying their desire for energetic measures may destroy the edifice that they have so carefully constructed.

It is for this reason that enthusiasm may be considered with justice as an enemy of poise.

Those who act under the domination of an impulse born of a too-vivid impression are rarely in a state of mind that can be depended on to judge sanely and impartially. They nearly always overshoot the mark at which they aim. They are like runners dashing forward at such a high speed that they can not bring themselves to a sudden stop. Habitual enthusiasm is also the enemy of reflection. It is an obstacle to that reason from which proceed strong resolves, and one is often impelled, in observing people who are fired with too great an ardor, to thoughts of the fable of the burning straw.

A teacher, who inclined to the methods that consist of object lessons, one day asked two children to make a choice between two piles, one of straw, the other of wood. It is hardly necessary to add that while the size of the pile of straw was great that of the wood was hardly one-tenth of the volume.

The first child, when told to make his choice, took the mass of straw, which he set on fire easily enough, warming himself first from a respectful distance and then at close range, in proportion as the heat of the fire grew less.

In so doing he made great sport of his companion, who struggled meanwhile to set alight the pile of wood. But what was the outcome?

The huge mass of straw was soon burned out, while the wood, once lit, furnished a tranquil and steady flame, which the first child watched with envy while seated by the mass of cinders that alone remained of the vanished pile that he had chosen.

The man of real poise is like the child who, disclaiming the transitory blaze of the straw, prefers to work patiently at building a fire whose moderate heat will afford him a durable and useful warmth.

Let us then beware of sudden unreasoning enthusiasms. After the ephemeral flame of their first ardor has burned itself out we shall but find ourselves seated by the mass of ashes formed of our mistakes and our dead energies.

The rock on which so many abortive attempts are wrecked in the effort to achieve poise is a type of sentimentality peculiar to certain natures.

This state of mind is characterized by a craving for expansion, which is all the more irritating since the timidity of the person concerned prevents it from being satisfied.

In place of relying on themselves, feeling their disabilities and the lack of poise which prevents them from proper expression, such people try to make themselves understood by those who do not appreciate their feelings, without stopping to think that they have done nothing to make clear what they really need.

Such a chaotic state of mind, based on errors of judgment, is a very serious obstacle to the acquisition of poise.

This anxiety to communicate their feelings, always rendered ineffective by the difficulty of making the effort involved, gives rise in the long run to a species of misanthropy.

It is a matter of common knowledge that misanthropy urges those who suffer from it to fall back on themselves, and from this state to that of active hostility toward others the road is short, and timid people are rarely able to pull up before they have traversed it.

There comes to them from this intellectual solitude an unhappiness so profound that they are glad to be able to attribute to the mental inferiority of others the condition of moral isolation in which they live.

To insist that they are misunderstood, and to pride themselves on the fact, is the inevitable fate of those who never can summon up courage to undertake a battle against themselves.

It seems to them a thousand times easier to say: "These minds are too gross to comprehend mine," than to seek for a means of establishing an understanding with those whom they tax with ignorance and insensibility.

They might, perhaps, be convinced of the utility to them of divulging their feelings, could they be forced into a position where they had to defend their ideas or were compelled to put up a fight on behalf of their convictions.

In the ranks of the enemies of poise sullenness most certainly finds a place.

It is the fault of the feeble-spirited who have not the energy to affirm their sentiments or to make a plain statement of their convictions that they become incensed with those who oppose them.

In their case a good deal of false pride is present. They know themselves to be beaten and to be incapable of fighting, yet they are too vain to accept defeat. They refuse the sympathy that wounds them, and suffer the more from their inability to yield themselves to that good-will which would aid and comfort them.

From this mental conflict is born an irritation that manifests itself in the form of obstinate sullenness.

In other cases the same state of mind may produce radically different results.

Always obsessed by the fear of appearing ridiculous and by the no less vivid dread of seeming to be an object of sympathy, such people are often driven through lack of poise into extreme boastfulness.

No man who has poise will ever fall a victim to this misfortune.

He knows exactly what his capabilities are and he has no need to exaggerate his own abilities to impress his friends.

Poise calls for action, when this becomes necessary; but the man of resolve, being always prepared to do what is needful, considers mere boasting and bravado as something quite unworthy of him.

There are, however, certain extenuating circumstances in the cases of those timid people who take refuge in boasting. They are almost invariably the dupes of their own fancies, and for the moment really believe themselves to be capable of endeavors beset by difficulties, of the surmounting of which they understand nothing.

Nothing looks easier to duplicate than certain movements which are performed with apparent ease by experts.

Which of us has not been profoundly astonished at the enormous difficulty experienced in accomplishing some simple act of manual toil that we see performed without the least effort by a workman trained to this particular task?

What looks easier, for instance, than to plane a piece of wood or to dig up the ground?

Is it possible that the laborer, wheeling a barrow, really has to be possessed of skill or strength?

It hardly seems so. And yet the man who takes a plane in his hands for the first time will be astounded at the difficulty he experiences in approximating to the regularity and lightness of stroke that comes naturally to the carpenter.

The man who essays to dig a piece of ground or to wheel a barrow, will find himself making irregular ditches and traveling in zigzags, and all this at the expense of a hundred times the energy put forth by the workman who is accustomed to these particular forms of labor.

The person of timidity who boasts of his remarkable exploits is actuated, as a general rule, by sheer lack of experience.

His peculiar fault keeps him always in the background and prevents him from accomplishing any public action, and for this reason those efforts appear easy to him that he has never thought of attempting.

Further than this, aided by his false pride, he considers that his merits are easily greater than those of the people who are not able to understand him, and he is acting in perfect good faith when he professes to be able to accomplish what they can not.

Is it necessary to add that the ironical reception given to such exhibitions of boastfulness rouse in him a feeling of irritation which is all the greater for the fact that he does not openly show it?

The man of resolve will never experience these unpleasant emotions.

He knows exactly what he wants and what he can do. So we see him marching ahead steadily, his eyes fixed on the goal he has worked out for himself, paying no heed whatever to misleading suggestions, which cripple his breadth of soul and would in the end deprive him of that essential energy which is vital to him if he would preserve his even poise, the foundation of mental balance and the source of every real success in life.

CHAPTER III

WAR ON TIMIDITY

One can not be too insistent in asserting how harmful the lack of poise can be, and when once this weakness has reached the stage of timidity it may produce the most tragic consequences not only so far as the daily routine of our lives is concerned, but also with reference to our moral and physical equilibrium.

So, when the nervous system is constantly set on edge by the emotions to which this fault gives rise, it necessarily follows that all the faculties suffer in their turn.

This is particularly true of those who are constantly haunted by the fear of finding themselves in a condition of mental unpreparedness, to the extent that they prefer to remain in solitude and silence rather than to mingle in a world which really has too many other things to think of to concern itself with their acts or their opinions.

This morbid dread of becoming the subject of ridicule ends by creating a peculiar condition of mind of which, as we have already pointed out, egoism is the pivot.

In this way it is a common occurrence to see people of timidity paying exaggerated attention to the slightest changes in the condition of their health.

Such people by shutting themselves out from the world have reduced it to the circumference of their own personalities and everything which touches them necessarily assumes gigantic importance in their eyes.

The slightest opposition becomes for them a catastrophe. The smallest unpleasantness presents itself to them in the light of a tragic misfortune.

For this reason the lives of the timid become a succession of boredoms and of pains.

Even in those cases where no really unfortunate incident occurs, these people so exaggerate what actually does happen to them that the least little emotion causes them the most profound unhappiness.

On those days when nothing in particular happens they spend their time anticipating all sorts of disasters, including those which are not the least likely to happen. To them the tiniest cloud is an omen of a devastating storm.

When the sun is shining their timidity prevents them from exposing themselves to the heat of its rays.

The timid man, in his moral isolation, is like the hare, who, crouched in its form, sleeps with one eye open in constant terror of the passer-by or of the hunter.

It may be well to add that worry about oneself is invariably an accompaniment of all these troubles. People without poise are, with very few exceptions, egotists who exaggerate their own importance.

Moreover, they suffer keenly from the obscurity into which their defects have forced them as well as from dread of the alternatives presented to them, the making of an effort to escape this fate, an idea that fills them with horror, or the continuing to live in the unhappy condition that has spoiled existence for them through their own faults.

It is hardly then a matter for surprise that so many people who are thus mentally out of balance end by becoming neurotics or become a prey to those cerebral disorders that are, unfortunately, all too frequent.

This condition of solitude, at once deplored and self-imposed, has the still more serious disadvantage of leaving the mind, for lack of proper control, to the domination of the most false and exaggerated ideas.

It is a well-known fact that any force of exaggeration, however obvious, becomes less noticeable to us in proportion as it becomes more familiar.

It exists, in the last analysis, only by its comparative relation to other things.

It is certain that a child ten years old would seem very large if he were five feet high, whereas a man of that stature is considered a dwarf.

Among Oriental races a woman is generally classed as a blonde whose hair is not absolutely black.

Things only take their real appearance from a comparison with others of the same kind.

For all his science, an ethnologist, placed in front of a man of an unknown tribe, would be unable to say whether this man's stature were normal or below the average in relation to others of his race, since no information would be forthcoming as to this people's height or characteristics. It is, therefore, no matter for surprise that the timid man, shut in on himself and having no other horizon than the limited field of his own observations, is disposed to picture them in colors whose truth he can not verify, since the terms of comparison, vital to the accomplishment of his end, are not available to him.

It is, therefore, impossible for such a man not to become accustomed to the idea as it presents itself to him, to such an extent that he is quite unconscious of its successive changes in character.

Do we notice the growth of a child who is constantly with us until he reaches man's estate?

Can we measure the development of a blossom into the perfect flower?

Assuredly not, if we have lived daily in the company of the child and have glanced several times an hour at the blossom.

Both the one and the other will reach maturity

without being sensibly conscious of the fact that they are changing.

But if we go away from the child for a few months, if, in the interval, we see other children, we can form an estimate of his growth and can compare him mentally with the other children we have met.

The same is true of the flower. If other duties call us away for the moment from contemplating it, we will notice the progress of its unfolding and we will also be able to tell whether, in relation to that of other plants, it is quick, slow, or merely normal.

The man who is timid, be he never so observant, will derive no benefit from these observations, for he is quite unable to generalize and refers them all to a point of view which cramps them hopelessly and gives them a color that is, entirely false.

So, from the habit of thinking without any opposition, little by little he allows his ideas to become changed and distorted without any one's being able to advise him of the misconceptions which he keeps closely to himself.

It is for this reason that all timid people have a marked tendency to distort facts and to acquire false ideas.

It is often with perfect good faith that they affirm a thing which they believe sincerely, not having had the opportunity to control the successive changes which have transformed it absolutely from what it was at the outset.

It is a lucky day for timid people of this class when

fate prevents them from entering into competition with those who are possessed of poise.

Were these latter a hundred times weaker than they are they would still end by triumphing over their feeble antagonists.

It is above all in the affairs of ordinary every-day life that poise renders the most valuable service.

If it becomes a question of presenting or discussing a matter of business, the timid man, embarrassed by his own personality, begins to stammer, becomes confused, and can not recall a single argument. He finally abandons all the gain that he dreamed of making in order to put an end to the torments from which he suffers.

He is to be considered lucky if under the domination of the troubles in which he finds himself, he does not lose all faculty of speech.

This failing, so common among the timid, is a further cause of confusion to the victim.

At the bare idea that he may become the prey of such a calamity he unconsciously closes his lips and lowers the tones of his voice.

The man of poise, on the other hand, feels himself the more impelled to redouble his efforts in proportion to the need his cause has for being well defended.

He knows how to arrange his arguments, and to foresee those of his adversary, and, if he finds himself face to face with a statement which he can not refute, he will seek some means of softening the defeat or of changing the ground of the debate in such a way as to avoid confusion to himself.

In any event, such an occurrence will have no profound effect on him. Vanquished on one point, he will find the presence of mind to at once change the character of the discussion to questions which are at once familiar and favorable to him.

He who goes forth into life armed with poise has also the marked advantage over the timid that comes from superior health.

This phrase should not be the occasion for a smile. Timidity is a chronic cause of poor health in those who suffer from it.

Pushed to extremes, it is the source of a thousand nervous defects.

We have already touched on stammering.

Unreasonable blushing is another misfortune of the timid. In drawing the attention of one's opponents it betrays at once one's ideas and one's fears.

Fear of this uncomfortable blushing inhibits many people from making the most of themselves or from properly protecting their own interests.

The shame they feel on account of this inferiority leads them, as we have seen, to seek isolation in which hypochondria slowly grows on them, sure forerunner of that terrible neurasthenia of which the effects are so diverse and so disconcerting.

The man who was at the outset no more than timid, easily becomes transformed first into a misanthrope, then into a monomaniac tortured by a thousand physical inhibitions, such as the inability to hold a pen, to walk unaccompanied across an open space, to ride in a public conveyance, etc., etc.

It must not be forgotten that these crises of embarrassments always produce extreme emotion accompanied by palpitations whose frequent recurrence may lead to actual heart trouble.

All these disadvantages increase the sullenness of the timid, who are overcome by the sense of their own physical weakness, which they know has its origin in a condition of mind that they lack the power either to change or to abolish.

All these causes of physical inferiority are unknown to the man who appreciates the value of poise and puts it into practice.

Such a man has no fear of embarrassment in speaking. He is a stranger to the misery of aimless blushing. If he does not always emerge victorious from the oratorical combats in which he engages he at least has the satisfaction of acknowledging to himself that he has not been beaten easily or without a struggle. In short, misanthropy, neurasthenia, and all their attendant ills, are for him unknown ailments.

One can not be too watchful against the attacks of timidity, which, like a contaminated spring, poisons the entire existence of those who are unable to dam up its flow.

Among the martyrdoms which are caused by it must be counted indecision, which is one of its most frequent and most unhappy results.

The timid man can not stop at any point.

He vacillates unceasingly and takes turn by turn the most opposing viewpoints.

It is only fair to add that he rejects them all almost as soon as he has formed them.

His state of mind being always one of distrust of his own powers, it is impossible for him not to be afraid that he has made a mistake, if he is left to do his own thinking.

We have seen how his craving for sympathy, never satisfied, since he does not make it known, drives him ever into impotent rage, which throws him back on himself in scarcely concealed irritation, that alienates him from all sympathy and precludes all confidences.

It is rarely, therefore, that the timid person does not find himself isolated when facing the decisions of greater or less gravity that daily life makes necessary.

In terror of making a mistake that may lead to some change of course or give rise to the necessity of taking some definite action, he hesitates everlastingly.

If, driven into a corner by circumstances, he ends by making some decision, we may be sure that he will at once regret it and that, if the time still remains to him, he will modify it in some way, only to revert to it again a moment later.

His will is like a ball continually thrown to and fro by children. No sooner is it tossed in one direction than it is suddenly sent flying in another, to return finally to its starting-place at the moment when the players' weariness causes it to fall to the ground.

This particular state of mind is primarily due to two causes:

The desire for perfection that haunts all timid people.

The fear of making a mistake that arises from the habit of continually mistrusting one's own judgment.

There are many other causes, the analysis of which is far beyond the scope of this work, but every one of these can be referred to the two main issues we have defined. The desire for perfection is at once the result and the cause of most timidity.

While the man of resolve, relying on his experience, is able to perform his part in those normal exigencies that he is able to conceive of, the timid man, shut off by his defects from all practical knowledge of life, comes to grief by discovering something amiss with every course that he considers.

A familiar proverb tells us that everything has its good and its bad side.

The timid see only the latter when making the decisions that fate imposes on them.

They fall into despair at their inability to see the other side of things and their feeble will drives against solid obstacles like a car colliding with a block of granite.

The man of resolution, instead of yielding to despair, seeks to surmount such a difficulty by turning his car in another direction; but, if the new road shows him nothing but dangerous pitfalls, he will choose to go around the block and continue his journey, remembering it as a landmark for his return.

For this reason we shall find him well on his way toward his journey's end while the victim of timidity continues to exhaust himself by vain efforts, thankful enough if he is not permanently mired in some of the bogs into which he has imprudently ventured. This is a state of affairs of much more frequent occurrence than one might suppose. Timidity, as we have seen, often unites the boldest conceptions with complete inexperience, which does not permit of accurate judgment as to impossibilities.

This lack of knowledge of life is also the cause of a continual fear of making mistakes.

The man of resolution never suffers from this complaint.

Having taught himself the value of a ripened judgment, he is quick to recognize the advantage to be derived from any project. He weighs alternatives carefully and only makes his decisions on well-thought-out grounds, after sufficient reasoned reflection to make sure that he will have no cause for future regret.

We have already remarked that such forms of irresolution constituted a martyrdom. The word is by no means too strong. They are never-ending occasions for physical and moral torture.

They are to be met with in the most trivial details of every-day life.

The mere crossing of a street becomes, for the nervous man, an ever-recurring source of torment.

He is afraid to go forward at the proper moment, takes one step ahead and another back, looks despairingly at the line of vehicles that bars his way, and, when a momentary opening in this confronts him, takes so long to make up his mind that the opportunity of crossing is past before he has seized it.

Or again he may suddenly rush forward, without any regard for the danger to which he is exposed, hesitating suddenly when in the way of the vehicles that threaten him, and quite incapable of slipping past them, or of any quick or dexterous movement by which he may avoid them.

This little picture, despite its commonplace nature, is nevertheless a symbol.

In the crossings of life, as well as those of the streets, the man who is timid is at an immense disadvantage when compared with the man of poise.

The latter does not worry his head about the traffic that blocks his progress.

Aided by his will-power and by confidence in his judgment, he stands firmly awaiting the moment that affords him an opening. Then, with muscles tense and wits collected, he starts, and whether he darts ahead here, or glides adroitly there, he threads his way through the traffic and reaches his goal without having suffered from accident.

The troubles on which we have been dwelling are never his. His soul, dominated by a well-ordered will, by reason, and all the other good qualities we enumerated in the first chapter, is proof against all attacks of weakness.

In the event of his not possessing all these virtues, he has the wit to keep the thought of them always before him and to work hard to acquire them, so that he may become what, in modern parlance, we call "a force," that is to say one whose soul is virile enough to influence not only his mind, but even to liberate his body from the defects created in it by distrust of self.

But, it will be claimed, there are people who are born timid and who are quite unable to achieve the mastery of themselves.

Every human being can win the victory over himself. This we will prove conclusively in the pages that are to follow, dedicated to those who are desirous of arming themselves, in the great game

of life, with that master card which is named
POISE.

PART II

HOW TO ACQUIRE POISE

CHAPTER I

MODESTY AND EFFRONTERY CONTRASTED

"Never force your talents" a well-known writer has said. One always feels like crying this to those who, thinking to reach the goal of poise, fall into excess and develop effrontery and exaggeratedness.

Poise can not exist without coolness. We have seen that this quality is rarely met with in enthusiasts.

It is never found in those who have effrontery.

Poise does not consist in the species of ostentatious carelessness which essays to travel through life as a child might wander among hives of bees without taking any precautions against being stung.

Neither is it that false courage that drives one headlong into a conflict without any thought as to the blows likely to fall on the foolhardy person who has ventured into it.

The principle on which we must start is this: life is a battle in which strategy always has the advantage over blind courage.

Unfortunate is he who, by his boasting or his lack of generalship, decides on an attack for which he is not really prepared. However brave he may be he will infallibly find himself vanquished in a struggle in which everything has combined in advance to defeat him.

Boasting is not courage. Still less is it poise.

Poise is a power derived from the mastery of self. It inhibits all outward manifestations that are likely to result in giving information to strangers with regard to our real feelings.

Braggarts can not avoid this stumbling-block. They know nothing of the delights of contemplation, from which arise ripe resolutions that will be steadfastly followed.

With the noise of their boastings, with the shouting of their own braggart ineptitudes, they hypnotize themselves so thoroughly that they are quite unable to hear the counsel that sane wisdom whispers in their ears.

They are like the man in the eastern fable who was quite unable to follow a beaten path and was constantly wandering across the fields of his neighbors.

These detours were in general much longer than the direct road would have been, and he received a constant stream of abuse, to say nothing of blows, from the people whose crops he was ruining.

But he seemed quite insensible to assaults and insisted on following, across lots, a road which led nowhere.

It would be difficult to paint a more faithful

portrait. Like the peasant in the story, the man of effrontery is always wandering far from the common road, the tranquil peace of which he despises.

He delights in crossing land that he knows to be forbidden to him, seeks to force open gates that are closed at his approach, and, if he can not overcome the opposition of the porter, watches for the moment when an open window will permit him entrance into a house where he will be coldly, if not angrily, received.

What is the result of this?

Nothing favorable to his plans, one may be sure. People point him out. They fly from him, and were he the bearer of the most advantageous proposition, refuse to put any faith in his assertions as soon as they get to know him in the least.

Effrontery may sometimes impose on the innocent. But it is only a momentary deception, quickly dissipated the moment that time is given to estimate the emptiness of its claims.

There is another variety of effrontery that is comparable to the form of courage exhibited by the timorous who sing in a loud voice in order to lessen their terror and imagine that by so doing they give the illusion of bravery.

People of this sort talk very loudly, often contradicting themselves, and pass judgment on everything, dismissing the most difficult questions with only a passing thought, but remain silent and are put completely out of countenance as soon as one insists on their listening to reason, or when—in familiar language—they "meet their match."

The man of effrontery is a passionate devotee of bluff, and not only of that variety of which Jonathan Dick has said:

"It is a security discounted in advance."

A little further on he adds:

"Bluffers of the right sort are only so when the occasion demands it, in order to give the impression that the wished-for result has already been achieved.

"As soon as their credit is assured and appearances have become realities that allow them to establish themselves in positions of security they at once cease the effort to deceive."

Our author concludes:

"Bluff, to be successful, must never be founded on puerility or brag."

Now these two qualities are always to be met with in the doings of the man of effrontery, who only achieves by accident the goal he aims at, and then only in the most insecure way.

Drawbacks differing as to their causes, but equally unlucky as to their results, are born of the opposite fault—modesty.

It is high time to destroy the leniency shown

toward this defect that old-fashioned educators once decorated with the title of virtue.

Time has forged ahead, taking with it in its rapid course all forms of progress, which, in its turn, has made giant strides.

Ideas have changed materially. Modern life has to face emergencies formerly undreamed of, and those who still believe in the virtue of modesty are their own enemies, as well as those of the people whom they advise to cultivate it.

The case of this man is similar to that of many others, whose meaning has been undergoing a gradual change due to the erroneous interpretation that has deliberately been placed on it.

Modesty is very frequently nothing more than an evidence of incompetence.

It has rise in sentiments that the man who would be up to date must avoid at all hazards—distrust of self and hatred of exertion.

One rarely finds it in the man who is active and who knows his own worth. To revenge itself, it flourishes among the lazy, who try to save their pride and to conceal their secret irritation at the successes of others by assuming an humble attitude and exclaiming:

"Oh! I didn't care to do it!"

Or still more frequently:

"No, I haven't entered the lists. I am absolutely

without ambition!"

Under similar circumstances people who are unknown cry out, and with reason:

"Oh! I have a horror of publicity!"

This is simply a roundabout way of informing us that were it not for their retiring modesty, the hundred mouths of rumor would be shouting their praise.

Modesty is very rarely what it appears to be. As soon as it exhibits the form of a wise reserve it must be called by another name: prudence and self-justification.

The attitude of trying to keep one's actions from becoming known is not a laudable one, and can only be adopted as the result of a philosophy of inaction.

What treasures of knowledge would have remained unknown to us if all the scientists and all the men of genius had made a practice of modesty!

If our forefathers had been modest, when it was the fashion to be proud of this quality, our museums would be empty and only a few of the initiated would know that men of exceptional merit, which they had sedulously concealed, had written manuscripts which had never been published. The humility of the writers in such cases could be made to pay too severe a penalty.

No! Men who have merits are not modest! This false virtue is the prerogative of none but weak and irresolute hearts.

We should congratulate ourselves, while admitting these facts, that our forefathers were not so constituted, and that their faith in themselves, by giving them confidence in their own work, made it possible for them to hand these on to their descendants.

Of what use to us would it be to know that a poem of finer quality and more splendid fire than any we have ever read had once been written, if the modesty of its author had led him to keep it always in his pocket and it had finally vanished into the limbo of ignored and forgotten things?

It is then actually wrong to sing the praises of modesty, which is no more than distrust of oneself, egoism, and laziness.

The man who boasts of his modesty will feel no shame at producing nothing. He hides his ineptitude behind this convenient veil whose thickness allows him to hint of the existence of things which are nothing but figments of his imagination.

We might add that the man who proclaims his modesty enters the struggle with a decided handicap against him. The moment he begins to have doubts about his own powers he will be sure to find himself the prey of an unfortunate indecision, and that at the very moment when he is called on to perform some decisive action.

"One day," says an old writer, "three men, in the course of a climb up a mountain, found themselves confronted by a crevasse that they must cross.

"One of these was a timid man, another a boaster, and the third was possessed of a reasoned poise.

"The boaster made a jump without stopping to think and without taking the trouble to measure the gap. He plunged into it.

"The modest man then advanced, looked down into the gulf, then decided to make use of the irregularities in the surface of the chasm to reduce the width of the jump.

"He made several attempts to carry this out, but could hardly touch the edge before an instinctive movement of fear forced him back.

"He worked so hard and so long at this that he was quite tired out when he at last chose the moment for the decisive attempt. He jumped, indeed, but in such a half-hearted way that he merely touched the opposite face of the crevasse and fell to the bottom of the precipice alongside of the boaster.

"The third climber, who possessed the advantage of poise, had meanwhile been losing no time. He had mentally choked the width of the crevasse, had made a number of trial jumps to test his ability to clear it, and when, with a firm resolution to succeed, he reached the edge from which he must leap, his soul, fortified by the knowledge of his powers was fired with a single idea, the consciousness of his own agility and strength.

"By this means he, alone of the three, was able to cross the gulf in which his two companions had perished."

Effrontery and boastfulness have often another source. The shyness of those who suffer from timidity, by isolating them and denying them the means of expansion, prevents them from obtaining a real control over their feelings, which undergo a process of deterioration so slow that they do not notice it.

There are very few things to which we can not easily become accustomed, to the extent of a complete failure to notice their peculiarities, if their strangeness is only unfolded to us gradually.

A thousand things which shock us at the first blush take on the guise of every-day matters when once we have acquired the habit of familiarity with them.

The timid man, who will not openly acknowledge his feelings, is practically unable to take cognizance of their gradual transformation.

We may add that he is always prone to dream, and peoples his world involuntarily with imaginary utopias, which he begins by considering as desirable, then as possible, and finally as actually existing.

This is the starting-point of boastfulness. It partakes at once of falsity and of sincerity. The timid man loves to feel himself important, and he merely pities the people whom he considers incapable of understanding him. He is, nevertheless, sincere in his bravado, as his dreams entirely deceive him as to his real self.

In his solitary meditations he deliberately shakes off his own personality, as a butterfly abandons the shelter of its chrysalis, and, following the example of that gorgeous insect, he flies away on the wings of his dreams in the guise of the being that he imagines himself to have become.

This creature resembles him not at all. It is brave, courageous, eloquent. It accomplishes the most brilliant feats of daring.

In this way, just so soon as the timid man becomes intermittently a braggart, he commences to boast of exploits quite impossible of performance. We must remember, however, that it is not he who speaks, but merely the idealized ego which he invents because he is chagrined at being misunderstood.

Moral isolation is the parent of other curious phenomena. It imparts the gift of seeing things exactly as we would wish them to be, by clothing them little by little with a character entirely foreign to that which they really possess.

In "Timidity: How to Overcome It," we are told the following little personal anecdote of the Japanese philosopher Yoritomo:

"It was my misfortune as a child," says this ancient sage, "to be the victim of a serious illness which kept me confined to a bed and unable to move.

"I was not allowed to read and my only distraction was the study of the objects in my immediate neighborhood.

"The pattern of a screen made a particular impression on me with its clusters of flowers and its bouquets of roses.

"I passed hours in the contemplation of it.

"At first I merely followed the outlines with my eye, finding in them no more than an artistic reproduction of nature. But, little by little, the clusters of flowers were transformed into gardens, the rose-trees took on the imposing aspect of forests. In these gardens my dreams created a princess, and in the forest a company of warriors.

"Then the romance began.

"Every new line I observed became the pretext for creating a new character. The princess was very soon taken captive by a giant—whom I saw perfectly—and the warriors undertook the task of rescue.

"Every day a panorama moved before me of changing personalities, who reenacted the events of the story. Finally the obsession took such a strong hold of me that I began to talk about it in a manner that aroused the fears of my parents.

"The screen was banished from my room and when, a few days later, it was brought back for me to see, I was able to discover nothing more in it than the designs with which it was adorned."

This example, taken directly from life, shows us better than the most extended arguments the dangers of moral isolation.

By this we do not mean the isolation that is essential to concentration, the practice of which always leads to the most fruitful results.

We are speaking solely of the aloofness born of timidity or of exaggerated pride, which, in depriving us of contrary views, develops in us the propensity to see things from only one angle, which is always that which happens to flatter our vanity or please our tastes.

All those persons who suffer from this disease of the will, which deprives them of the ability of discussing things, may be compared to runners who have neglected to ascertain the limits of their race.

Like the latter, they keep running round the same track without any means of discovering when they are nearing the goal.

Instead of stopping, when they have reached it, they keep running forward and the monotony of their efforts, coupled with the fever-heat engendered by their exertions, very soon causes them to view the objects that they keep passing and passing under a deformed and distorted aspect.

The man of reason, on the other hand, runs with the single purpose in his mind of reaching the winning-post. He studiously avoids taking his eyes off the goal, which he has carefully located in advance, and takes pains to note the moment when he is nearing it, so as to run no risks of making his spurt too soon.

It is a matter of frequent observation that timidity often voluntarily assumes the role of effrontery, from very despair of successfully accomplishing the task it is ambitious to perform.

Illustrious examples of this contention are not lacking. Rousseau, who was a coward of the greatest hardihood, says in his *Confessions* :

"My foolish and unreasoning fear, that I was quite unable to overcome, of perpetrating some breach of good manners led me to assume the attitude of caring nothing for the niceties of life."

A little further on, he adds:

"I was made a cynic by shyness. I posed as a despiser of the politeness I did not know how to practice."

This is a much more frequent cause than one might think of the exhibition of an effrontery which is apparently deliberate and intentional.

The timid man, feeling himself awkward and clownish when performing the usual acts of courtesy, assumes the attitude of caring nothing for them and of avoiding them deliberately, while all the while he is tortured by the inability to perform them without seeming ridiculous.

But the onlooker is not deceived. The outward appearance of cynicism often conceals an inward sensitiveness of soul that is quite obvious, and the actor makes so poor a hand at identifying himself with the character he would assume that it is clearly evident he is only playing a part.

The conflict of diametrically opposing forces shows itself plainly in his attitude which vacillates between the stiffest formality and the easiest assurance.

The awkwardness that is the bugbear of the timid shows itself even beneath their work of cynicism, and the very effort accuses them, no less than their flighty and unreasoning conversation and their gestures, now exaggerated and now repressed, all of which make up a whole that entirely fails to give an impression of harmony.

And what possible harmony can there be between a soul and a body that are completely out of accord with each other?

Should it be asked what the difference is between presumption or effrontery and the poise that we have in mind, this simple illustration should be illuminating.

Effrontery, bravado, and exaggeration are qualities that are shown by those who exceed their own capacity without giving the question a thought.

Poise is the virtue which gives us the strength of mind to analyze the possibilities that are dominant within us, to cultivate them, and to strengthen them in every possible way before undertaking an enterprise which is likely to call them into play.

Real poise has no bluster about it. It has a good deal in it of self-possession, the discretion belonging to which is one of its marked characteristics.

Repression of our outward movements enables us to achieve that control over our emotions which makes a perfect cloak for our intentions, and leaves our opponents in perplexity as to how to attack the fortress that they wish to conquer.

It is, therefore, between modesty and effrontery, both equally prejudicial to success, that poise must naturally be placed.

But, it will be objected, all the world does not possess this gift of poise. Are those who do not share it to be forever denied all chance of success?

Not so! It is open to all the world to acquire this gift, and if the chapters following this are read with care it will be seen that it is something that can be cultivated, so that it can be gradually perfected and carried about with one as the germ of every sort of success, the happy issue of which depends on a thorough realization of one's own merits and the honorable ambition to accomplish a task that has been prudently planned and bravely carried to an end.

CHAPTER II

PHYSICAL EXERCISES TO ACQUIRE POISE

Before preparing oneself by the exercise of reasoning and will-power for the acquisition of poise, it is vitally necessary to make oneself physically fit for the effort to be undertaken.

One should begin with this fundamental principle:

Timidity being a disease one must treat it just as one would any other illness.

Like all other physical maladies it is sure to be the cause of loss of social prestige to those who suffer from it.

It must then be combated in the same way as any other infirmity of long standing that threatens to ruin the life of the sufferer.

It is a grave mistake to consider it merely a mental ailment that can be alleviated by nothing but psychological treatment.

One's nervous condition plays a very large part in the conquest of poise.

We must, therefore, watch most carefully over the good health of the body before taking any measures whatever to abolish a condition of affairs that has been engendered by physical weakness and that will be fostered by it unless such weakness can be eradicated or more or less dissipated and ameliorated by a thousand little daily acts of care.

It must be understood that we are not now speaking of medical treatment. We have reference merely to that common-sense hygiene which has become more or less a part of modern existence, and the daily practice of which, while firmly establishing the health, has at the same time an undoubted reflex action on the mind. It is a well-known fact that energy is never found in a weakened body, and that people who are suffering are clearly marked down to become the prey of those wasting diseases, whose names, all more or less fantastic, may be classed as a whole under the general heading of "nervous maladies."

To enumerate them is superfluous and unnecessary. Lack of poise gives rise to all sorts of weaknesses, which are given the names of nervous diseases and finally become classed in the category of phobias, of which the starting-point is always a habit of fear due to excess of timidity. This morbid disposition is the parent of a continual apprehensiveness which is shown on all sorts of occasions.

The man who has the space phobia is quite unable to cross an open space unless he is supported or, at the very least, accompanied.

Claustrophobia is the malady of those who have a horror of close quarters from which they can not easily make their escape.

Writers' cramp is nothing in the world but one of these exaggerated nervous terrors.

Erythrophobia, that is to say the habit of inopportune and constant blushing, is another of the commonest forms of excessive timidity.

Stammering is another of the tortures that people of poise do not experience, except in those cases where it is caused by a physical malformation.

All these maladies attack only the timid.

There are many others, less serious in their nature, such as indecision, exaggerated scrupulousness, extreme pliability, hypochondria. All of these should be ruthlessly suppressed the moment we become aware of them, for they are one and all the forerunners of that mentally diseased condition which gives rise to the phobias of which we have just been speaking.

To those who would seriously devote themselves to the cultivation of poise it is, therefore, a vital necessity to be in a condition of perfect health. It would be a misfortune, indeed, for them to find themselves balked in their progress toward acquiring this quality by anxieties regarding the condition of their bodies.

Any indisposition, not to mention actual diseases, has a tendency to inhibit all initiative.

There is no room for doubt that a physical ailment by attracting to itself the attention of the person who is attacked by it, prevents him from giving the proper amount of energy to whatever he may be engaged on.

He thinks about nothing but his malady and quite forgets to take the exercises that would enable him to alter his condition, to change his actions, and even to make over his thoughts.

His thoughts above all. Physical well-being has an undeniable influence on one's mental health.

One very rarely sees a sick person who is happy. Even those who are endowed with great force of character lose, under the burden of their sufferings, part of their firmness of soul and of their legitimate ambition.

A very scientific force of hygiene is particularly recommended. Excessive measures of any sort must be avoided for various reasons:

(1) They are antagonistic to the maintenance of a perfect physical equilibrium.

(2) They will inevitably grow to dominate the mind unduly.

When we speak of excesses, we intend to include those undertaken in the way of work no less than those which are the outcome of the search for pleasure.

Nevertheless we will hasten to add that these last are much the more to be feared.

What can be expected, for instance, from a man who has passed a night in debauchery?

Morning finds him a weakling, good for nothing, and incapable of making the slightest effort that calls for energy.

He is lucky, indeed, if his excesses have no disastrous results that will destroy his happiness or his good name.

The fear of complications that may be the outcome of his gross pleasures soon begins to haunt him and to usurp in his mind the place of nobler and more useful impulses.

As to his health, it is hardly necessary for us to insist on the disorder that such habits must necessarily produce.

The least misfortune that he can look for is a profound lassitude and a desire for rest which is the enemy of all virile effort.

The same thing is true of the man who indulges too freely in the pleasures of the table. The work of digestion leaves him in an exhausted condition and with a craving for repose that very soon results in a complete lack of moral tone.

Even supposing that his daily routine consists of two principal meals, and of two others of less importance, it will be easily understood that the man who loads down his stomach with such a large amount of continuous work will not be very apt to adapt himself readily to matters of a wholly different kind.

To avoid pain, to sit inert, like a gorged animal, without attempting to think, is the sole desire of the gluttons who are wearied by every repeated excess.

The same reasoning could be applied to the lazy, who suffer in health from indulgence in their favorite vice.

It can not be disputed that lack of exercise is the cause of ailments that have a marked effect on the moral character.

Since physical laziness always goes hand in hand with mental apathy, it follows that a dread of exerting oneself is always to be found coupled with a hatred of being forced to think.

It is, therefore, essential for the man who would acquire poise to fortify himself in advance against physical weaknesses which, by undermining his will-power, will soon furnish him with the most plausible reasons for losing interest in the steady application that is needed for accomplishing his purpose.

In achieving the conquest of poise certain physical exercises, practiced every day, and vigorously followed out, will be found of considerable help.

Before discussing the practical methods which are at once their starting-point and their result, we will consider in turn the series of exercises that must be performed each day in order to keep oneself in the condition of physical well-being which allows of the accomplishment of moral reform.

CHAPTER III

FOUR SERIES OF PHYSICAL EXERCISES

FIRST SERIES—BREATHING

The point of departure for the cultivation of poise, like that of everything else in fact, must be a well-ordered system of hygiene, far removed from excess, and insisting only on the points we have already indicated.

Without wishing to fall into the well-known error of so many modern teachers, who assign an exaggerated importance to breathing exercises, we must, nevertheless, admit the great role that respiration plays in physical balance.

We are now speaking, understand, of methodical breathing, we might almost term it "reasoned" breathing.

Every one, of course, breathes without being aware of it from the moment of his birth to the hour of his death, but very few people are aware how to increase the power and to enlarge the capacity of their lungs.

Nevertheless, on these conditions it is that activity depends, as well as the health and the energy that enables us to consecrate ourselves to the pursuit of a definite aim.

Without having to lay claim to a vast knowledge of medicine one can discover that all repeated exercise tends to strengthen the organ that is employed.

Thus, well-directed and carefully practiced breathing gives the heart a stronger beat and facilitates the action of the lungs.

From these arises a general feeling of physical well-being, which tends to the preservation of good health and stores up the energy we need to carry out our resolves.

It is, then, advisable to devote several minutes every day to breathing exercises, not merely automatic, but purposeful and under thorough control.

To accomplish this there are two methods.

The first, very easy of comprehension, is to lie down on one's back and to breathe deeply with the mouth closed and the nostrils dilated.

As much air as can be held must be taken into the lungs, then the mouth must be opened and the air must be allowed to escape gradually.

During this operation one should pay particular attention to expanding the walls of the chest, while flattening the stomach.

About twenty deep respirations are required to accomplish the desired effect.

Little by little the lungs will dilate and one will

unconsciously increase the length of the inspiration and the slowness with which the air is expelled.

The second method consists in standing erect, with the head thrown slightly back. The lungs should then be filled with air and one should count mentally up to five or even ten before exhaling the air that has been breathed in.

It is advisable that when exhaling one should utter a continuous hum, which must be absolutely free from trembling when one has practiced it properly.

People who have practiced this exercise have often stated that this method of breathing has been of great help to them when much fatigued as well as a first-class stimulus in moments when all their physical powers were to be called into play.

A well-known college professor has assured us that every day, before giving his lectures, he makes use of this exercise. He claims that he has thus gained a freedom of breathing the good effects of which are manifest in the facility with which he is able to give his lecture and in his general feeling of ease. Rendered quite free from any suspicion of nervousness, he feels that he is completely master of himself and in a fit state of moral and physical health to employ the poise that is essential to the man who has to instruct and to convince others.

Deep breathing has the further advantage of developing the lungs, of strengthening them, and at the same time of making their ordinary functioning more regular.

The man who practices this exercise will have much less propensity to get out of breath. This will be a great assistance to those timid people who are disconcerted by trifles and who, at the least little occurrence, become so much affected by emotion that they experience a sensible acceleration of the action of the heart.

Palpitation can not take place without causing us physical discomfort, and this condition is a serious stumbling-block in the way of the acquisition of poise, for, in view of the great stress the man of timidity lays on the opinion of others, he will be apprehensive of giving them any inkling of his distress, and yet his difficulty in breathing will be bound to reveal it.

The exercise of which we have been speaking should be performed with care twice a day.

For those whose leisure hours are few it can be accomplished without losing any of the time which is already preempted by other things.

It is merely a question of remembering it as soon as one wakes in the morning and of never forgetting it before one falls asleep at night.

The few minutes between the moment that one wakes and the time one gets out of bed can be most profitably employed in this way.

The same thing is true at night.

If the occupations of the day and of the evening leave us no time to devote to this exercise, we can always go through it in the moments between retiring to bed and falling asleep.

It will thus be seen that there is really no valid excuse for not undertaking this practice, whose effects will certainly be most beneficial.

SECOND SERIES—TRAINING OF THE EYE

But our physical efforts must not stop here.

It is more than necessary that we should make others feel the effects of the mastery that we are slowly acquiring over ourselves.

The eye is an invaluable assistant to the man who is studying to acquire poise.

It is not necessary here, in connection with the magnetic properties of the eye, to enter into a digression too extensive for the scope of this book, but we can not neglect this one more-than-important factor altogether.

We are speaking now not only of the power in the gaze of others but of that of our own eyes in relation to our associates.

We must do our best, in fine, to develop the power of our gaze, while studying to fortify ourselves against the influence brought to bear on us in this direction by others.

One frequently notices, especially in the case of people who are timid, a propensity to lose their powers of resistance with those who are able to fix them with a steady stare.

One has often seen people who lack will-power emerging completely upset from the grueling of an interview in which they have admitted everything that they had most fervently resolved never to disclose.

A superior force has dominated them to such an extent that they have found it impossible to conduct the discussion in the way they had planned to do it.

The man who is in earnest about acquiring poise must, then, be on his guard against betraying himself under the magnetism of some one else's gaze.

At the same time he must cultivate his own powers of the eye, so that he, too, can possess that ability against which, in others, he must be careful to protect himself, and can utilize it for his own ends.

The first principle is to avoid looking directly into the pupils of one's interlocutor.

This is the only way in which a beginner can avoid being affected by the magnetism of the gaze.

By this word magnetism we have in mind nothing verging in the least on the supernatural.

We have reference only to the well-known physical discomfort experienced by those who have not yet become masters of poise when meeting a steady stare.

Its effect is so strong that, in the majority of cases, the timid are quite unable to endure it. They stammer, lose their presence of mind, and finally reveal everything they are asked to tell, if only to escape from the tyranny of the gaze which seems to go right through them and to dictate the words that they must utter.

One must be careful, then, not to allow oneself to become swayed by the gaze of another. But since it would seem ridiculous to keep one's eyes constantly lowered, and is impolite to allow them to wander from the face of the person with whom one is speaking, one can escape the magnetic effect of his pupils by looking steadily at the bridge of his nose directly between his eyes.

When first practicing this one must be careful not to look too fixedly, for the eye has not yet acquired the necessary muscular power, and one will quickly find oneself fascinated instead of dominating.

But this method is an absolute safeguard, if one does not stare too fixedly.

It must not be forgotten that this spot is known as the "magnetic point."

In the case of those who have made no study of the power of the eye, and particularly of those who are lacking in poise, this method of looking steadily at the bridge of the other's nose, while not having any marked effect on him, will save them from becoming the tools of his will.

Certain easy exercises will be found most useful in

arriving at the possession of the first notions of this art, so indispensable in the ordinary applications of poise.

One good way is to look steadily, for several seconds at first and later on for several minutes at a time, at some object so small that the eye can remain fixed on it without discomfort.

For the latter reason it is better to choose something dark. A brilliant object will much more readily cause fatigue and dizziness.

We have said for several seconds to begin with. It will be found a matter of sufficient difficulty to keep one's gaze fixed for much longer than this, when one is unaccustomed to this sort of exercise.

One should endeavor to keep the two eyes open without winking. One should not open them too wide nor yet close them. The head should be kept steady and the pupils motionless.

If this attempt causes the least wandering of the gaze or the slightest winking of the eyes, it must be begun over again.

It is for this reason that at the start it will be found difficult to keep it up for more than a few seconds.

After resting awhile one should repeat the exercise afresh, until the time comes when one can concentrate one's gaze in this way for at least four or five minutes of perfect fixity.

In order to keep count of the time that is passing, as well as to keep control of one's will-power, it is advisable to count aloud in such a way that approximately one second elapses between the naming of every two numbers.

When once fixity of gaze has been acquired, one can essay various other exercises, such as concentrating the eyes on an object and turning the head slowly to one side and the other without removing one's gaze from this point for a moment.

It is not until one is very certain that the muscles of the eye have been thoroughly trained that one should undertake the mirror test.

To do this, one must take up a position in front of a glass and fix one's gaze on one's own pupils for a time. Then one must transfer it to the bridge of the nose, between the two eyes, and must strive to keep it there immovably.

At first this exercise will not be found as easy as one might suppose. The magnetic power of the pupils is great and one will experience some slight difficulty in breaking away from it.

For this reason it is a good plan to count out loud slowly up to a predetermined number, at which point the gaze should be at once transferred to the bridge of the nose.

These exercises of the eye will be found particularly beneficial for people who are desirous of acquiring poise, as aside from the advantages we have specified, they have the effect of strengthening the will-power, which will be found to have materially gained by this means.

When the desired result appears to have been accomplished and one feels oneself strong enough to meet or to avoid another person's eye, while at the same time one is conscious that one can dominate with one's own, it will be well to experiment on the people with whom one is closely associated.

One can thus become accustomed, little by little, to control one's gaze, to force an estimate of its influence, and to neutralize the effect of that of other people.

THIRD SERIES—THE MOTIONS, THE CARRIAGE

Another highly important point in the conquest of poise is the struggle against awkwardness, which is at once the parent and the offspring of timidity.

Let us make ourselves clear.

Many people only lack poise because they fear ridicule of their obvious embarrassment and of the awkward hesitation of their movements.

Others fall into this embarrassment as the result of exhibitions of clumsiness in which they cover themselves with ridicule. The terror of renewing their moments of torture drives them into a reserve, from which they only emerge with a constraint so evident that it is reflected in their gestures, the evidences of a deplorable awkwardness.

It is exceedingly simple to find a remedy for these unpleasant conditions. One must make up one's mind to combat their exhibitions of weakness by determining to acquire ease of movement.

We have all noticed that awkwardness occurs only in public.

The most embarrassed person in the world carries himself, when alone, in a fashion quite foreign to that which is the regret of his friends.

It may happen, however, that awkwardness too long allowed to become a habit will have a disastrous effect on our daily actions, and that the person who is lacking in poise will end by keeping up, even in private, the awkward gestures and uncouth movements that cause him eternal shame at his own expense.

In such a case a cure will be a little more difficult to effect, but it can be arrived at, without a shadow of doubt, if our advice is faithfully followed out.

It is an obvious truth that the repetition of any act diminishes the emotion it gave rise to in us at the first performance.

Physical exercises are then in order, to achieve for us suppleness of movement and to extend its scope.

Every morning, after our breathing exercises (which can be performed in bed between the moment of waking and that of getting up, according to our advice to those whose time is limited) it is absolutely necessary to devote five minutes to bodily exercises, the object of which is the acquirement of an easy carriage from the frequent repetition of certain movements.

For instance, one should endeavor to expand the chest as far as possible, while throwing back the head and extending the arms, not by jerky movements but by a wide and rhythmical sweep, which should be every day made a little more extended.

While doing this one should hollow the back so that it becomes a perfect arch.

Then one should walk up and down the room, endeavoring to keep one's steps of even length and one's body erect.

One should never allow these daily exercises to go unperformed on the pretext of lack of time.

Five minutes of deep breathing and five minutes to practice the other movements advised will be sufficient, if one performs these tasks every day with regularity and conscientiousness.

The speaking exercises, to which we shall now refer can be carried out while we are dressing.

Choose a phrase, a short one to start with, and longer as you progress, and repeat it in front of the glass while observing yourself carefully, to be sure that your face shows no sign of embarrassment and that you do not stammer or hesitate in any way.

If the words do not come out clearly, you must

make an immediate stop and go doggedly back to the beginning of your phrase, until you are able to enunciate it with mechanical accuracy and without a single sign of hesitation.

You must study to avoid all the jerky and abrupt movements which disfigure the address of the timid and deprive them of all the assurance that they should possess, for the reason that they can not help paying attention to their own lack of composure.

Finally, from the moment of rising, as well as when brushing his hair, tying his necktie, or putting on his clothes, the man who desires to acquire poise will watch himself narrowly, with a view to making his movements more supple and to invest them with grace.

Once in the street, he will not forget to carry his head erect, without exaggerating the pose, and will always walk with a firm step without looking directly ahead of him.

If this attitude is a difficult one for him when commencing, he can, at the start, assign a certain time for observing this position, and gradually increase its length, until he feels no further inconvenience.

The feeling of obvious awkwardness is a large factor in the lack of poise.

It is then a matter of great importance to modify one's outward carriage, while at the same time applying oneself to the conquest of one's soul, so as to achieve the object not only of actually becoming a man who must be reckoned with, but of impressing every one with what one is, and what one is worth.

FOURTH SERIES—SPEAKING EXERCISES

Is it really necessary to point out what a weight readiness of speech has in bringing about the success of any undertaking?

The man who can make a clever and forceful speech will always convince his hearers, whatever may be the cause he pleads.

Do we not see criminals acquitted every day solely because of the eloquence of their lawyers?

Have we not often been witnesses to the defeat of entirely honest people who, from lack of ability to put up a good argument, allow themselves to be convicted of negligence or of carelessness, if of nothing worse?

Eloquence, or at least a certain facility of speech, is one of the gifts of the man of poise.

One reason for this is that his mind is always fixed on the object he wishes to attain by his arguments, which eliminates all wandering of the thoughts.

But there is another reason, a purely physical one. The emotions experienced by the timid are quite unknown to him and he is not the victim of any of the physical inhibitions which, in affecting the clearness of their powers of speech, tend to reduce them to confusion.

Stammering, stuttering, and all the other ordinary disabilities of the speaker, can almost without exception be attributed to timidity and to the nervousness of which it is the cause.

We shall see in the next chapter how these defects can be cured.

In this, which is devoted specially to physical exercises, we will give the mechanical means for overcoming these grave defects.

Just as soon as the difficulties of utterance have been overcome, and one is no longer in terror of falling into a laughable blunder, and thus has no further reason to fear, when undertaking to speak, that one will be made fun of because the object of disconcerting mockery, one's ideas will cease to be dammed up by this haunting dread and can take shape in one's brain just as fast as one expresses them.

Clearness of conception will be reflected in that of what we say, and poise will soon manifest itself in the manner of the man who no longer feels himself to be the object of ill-natured laughter.

One should set oneself then every morning to the performance of exercises consisting of opening the mouth as wide as one possibly can and then shutting it, to open it once more to its fullest extent, and so on until one becomes fatigued.

This exercise is designed to cover the well-known

difficulty of those who speak infrequently and which is familiarly known as "heavy jaw."

One should next endeavor to pronounce every consonant with the utmost distinctness.

If certain consonants, as *s*, for example, or *ch*, are not enunciated clearly, one should keep at it until one pronounces them satisfactorily.

Now one should construct short sentences containing as many difficult consonants as possible.

Next we should apply ourselves to declaiming longer sentences.

It will be of help to have these sentences constitute an affirmation of will-power and of poise.

For example: "I can express myself with the greatest possible facility, because timidity and embarrassment are complete strangers to me."

Or again: "I am a master of the art of clothing my thoughts in elegant and illuminating phrases, because stammering, stuttering, and all the other misfortunes that oppress the timid, are to me unknown quantities."

We can not insist too strongly on the cumulative effect of words which are constantly repeated. It is a good thing to impress oneself with forceful ideas that make for courage and for achievement.

Distrust of self being the principal defect of the timid, the man who would acquire poise must bend every effort to banishing it from his thoughts.

The repetition of these sentences, by building up conviction, will undoubtedly end by creating a confidence in oneself that will at first be hesitating, but will gradually acquire force. This is a great step in advance on the road toward poise.

We are discussing, it should be understood, only such cases of difficulty in speaking as are directly traceable to an inherent timidity.

If the inability to speak clearly comes from a physical malformation it should at once be brought to the attention of a specialist.

It is well recognized that, in the majority of cases, those defects are the consequences of timidity, when they are not its direct cause.

In combating them, then, with every means at his disposal, the man who desires to acquire poise will prove the logicality of his mind. It is a well-known axiom that effects are produced by causes, and *vice versa*.

Thus, in the case we are considering, timidity either causes the difficulty in speaking or is caused by it. In the first condition as well as in the second, the disappearance of the one trouble depends on the eradication of the other.

CHAPTER IV

PRACTICAL EXERCISES FOR OBTAINING POISE

COMPOSURE

One of the essential conditions of acquiring poise is to familiarize oneself with the habit of composure.

Timid people know nothing of its advantages. They are always ill at ease, fearful, devoured by dread of other people's censures, and completely upset by the idea of the least initiative.

Their mania leads them to exaggerate the smallest incident. A trifle puts them in a panic, and at the mere notion that strangers have perceived this they become quite out of countenance and are possessed by but one idea, to avoid by flight the repetition of such unpleasant emotions.

A quite useless attempt, for in whatever retirement people who lack poise may live, they will find themselves certainly the victims of the small embarrassments of every-day life, which, in their eyes, will soon take on the guise of disasters.

Composure should, then, be the first achievement in the way of self-conquest to be aimed at by the man who is desirous of attaining poise.

But, it will be objected, composure is a condition

that is not familiar to everybody. It is a question of temperament and of disposition. Every one who wishes for it can not attain to it.

This is an error. In order to possess composure, that is to say the first step in the mastery of self which enables one to judge of the proportions of things, it must be achieved, or developed, if we happen to be naturally inclined thereto.

To accomplish this, deep-breathing exercises are often recommended by the philosophers of the new school.

They advise those who are desirous of cultivating it to make no resolution, to commit themselves to no impulsive action, without first withdrawing into themselves and taking five or six deep breaths in the manner we have described in the preceding chapter.

This has the physical effect of reducing the speed with which the heart beats and, as a result, of relaxing the mind and quieting one's nerves.

During the two or three minutes thus employed one's enthusiasm wanes and one's ideas take on a less confused form. In a word, unreasoning impulses no longer fill the brain to the extent of inhibiting the entrance of sober second thought.

But this is only an adventitious means of prevention. We will now speak of those which should become a matter of daily practice and whose frequent repetition will lead to the poise we seek.

Every one whose profession makes it necessary to cultivate his memory recognizes the importance of studying at night. Phrases learned just before going to sleep fix themselves more readily in the mind. They remain latent in the brain and spring up anew in the morning without calling for much trouble to revive them.

For this reason it is well to retire to rest in a mental attitude of deliberate calm, repressing every sort of jerky movement and constraining oneself to lie perfectly quiet.

At the same time one should keep on repeating these words:

"I am composed. I propose to be composed. I am composed!"

The constant reiteration of these words constitute a species of suggestion, and peace will steal gradually into our souls and will permit us to think quietly, without the risk of becoming entangled in disordered fancies, or, what is far worse, falling a prey to vain and unavailing regrets.

Those who doubt the efficacy of this proceeding can be readily convinced by proving to them the tremendous power of mere words.

Certain of these electrify us. Such words as patriotism, revolt, blood, always produce in us an emotion of enthusiasm or disgust.

Others again are productive of color, and one must admit that the constant repetition of an assurance ultimately leads to the creation of the condition that it pictures to us.

But to make the assertion to oneself, "I am composed," is not all that is necessary. One must prove to oneself that one is not glossing over the truth.

The readiest means of accomplishing this, which is open to every one who has any regular interests, is to mentally review the words and the actions of the day, and to pass judgment on them from the point of view of the quality one is striving to attain.

DAILY SELF-EXAMINATION

One should convince oneself as soon as possible of the truth of the fact that sincerity toward oneself is a large factor in attaining that firmness of judgment that must be cultivated by the man who is in search of poise.

In order to reach this condition nothing is more easy than to pass in mental review, every evening, the events that have marked the day that has passed.

In a word, one should strive to relive it, honestly confessing to oneself all the mistakes that have crept into it.

Every unfortunate speech should be recalled. One should formulate fresh replies, that lack of poise did not permit us to make at the time, so that under similar circumstances we may not be again caught at a disadvantage.

The witty name of "doorstep repartee" has been given to these answers which one makes as afterthoughts, with the idea of expressing the embarrassment of the man who can find no arguments until he finds himself beyond the reach of his opponents. It is after one has gone out, when one is on the doorstep, that one suddenly recognizes what one ought to have said, and finds the phrases that one should have used, the exact retort that one might have hurled at one's antagonist.

The man who has acquired poise should still accustom himself to practice this force of mental gymnastics when making his daily self-examination.

It will strengthen him for future contests by teaching him just how to conduct himself.

He must be always on his guard against one of the obsessions that too often afflict the timid—the mania for extremes.

The nature of a timid person is essentially artificial. His character is unequal.

He yearns for perfection, yet it is painful for him to meet it in others. He suffers also because he has failed to acquire it himself.

Sometimes he is his own most severe judge and then on other occasions he is grossly indulgent to his faults.

His isolation causes him to construct ideals that can not possibly be realized in ordinary life. But he is more than ready to blame those who fall short of them, while making no effort to duplicate their struggles.

He makes the sad mistake, as we have seen in the chapter on effrontery, of taking all his chimeras for realities and is angry at his inability to make other people see them in the same light.

He is, moreover, of a very trustful disposition and prone to the making of confidences. But when he attempts them his infirmity prevents him and he suffers under the inhibition.

All his mental processes, as we have seen, tend toward hypochondria, unless his sense of truth can be called into play.

One can easily see then that this daily self-examination can be made quite a difficult affair by all these conflicting tendencies.

It is for this very reason that it is so necessary that this examination should be rigorously undertaken every day and with all the good faith of which we are possessed.

It is because they do not ignore their own weaknesses that the men endowed with poise become what one has psychologically termed "forces," that is to say people who are masters of a power that renders them superior to the rest of the world.

RESOLUTION

After as minute and as honest an examination as we can make of our own actions, it will be of great benefit to make definite resolutions for the morrow.

This is a matter of great importance.

The timid man, by seriously resolving to perform the actions that he ought and by planning the accomplishment of some definite step, will unconsciously strengthen his own will-power.

He will increase it still more by making up his mind to leave no stone unturned to conquer himself.

For instance, he proposes to make a certain journey, or to pay a certain call, which he dreads very much, and falls asleep while repeating to himself: "To-morrow I will go there! I will carry the thing through with assurance!"

Conceding the magnetic power of words, the acquisition of courage and of confidence are necessary corollaries.

Ideas impressed on the mind at the moment that one is falling asleep develop during the night by a species of incubation, and on the morrow present themselves to us quite naturally in the guise of a duty much less hard to perform than we had imagined.

In the case where such a resolution awakens an unpleasant emotion in the hearts of the timid, they should repeat earnestly the sentences that tend to composure and should seek the aid of the means we have indicated for attaining it.

PREPARATION

In order to strengthen one's resolution it is a good thing every morning to map out one's day, for the purpose of acquiring poise.

All one's combinations should be worked out with this valuable conquest in mind.

After having committed oneself to a definite plan, one should analyze each one of the proposed steps, carefully taking into account all the peculiarities that are likely to characterize them.

If one is to have an interview, one should carefully prepare one's introductory remarks, paying particular attention to one's line of action, to one's method of presentation, and the words on which one relies to obtain an affirmative reply to one's request.

One should take the precaution to have one's speeches mentally prepared in advance, so as to be able to deliver them in such a speedy and convincing fashion that one does not find oneself in a state of embarrassment fatal to recollecting them.

It is better to make them as short as possible. One is then much less likely to become confused and will not be so much in dread of stammering or stuttering, which are always accompaniments of the fear of being left without an idea of what to say next.

Besides this, long speeches are always irritating, and it is a sign of great lack of address to allow oneself to acquire the reputation of being a bore.

To make sure of one's facial expression and gestures it may be well to repeat one's speeches in front of a mirror.

One can then enact one's entry into the room in such a way as to foresee even the most insignificant details, so that the fear of making a failure at the start will no longer have a bad effect on one.

We have heard of a man who was so lacking in poise that he lost his situation because, when summoned by his chief, he became so confused that he forgot to leave his streaming umbrella in the outer office.

It was an extremely wet day, and the unfortunate man, instead of being able to plead his cause effectively, became hopelessly embarrassed at perceiving his mistake, the results of which, it is needless to state, were by no means to the benefit of the floor.

His despair at the sight of the rivulets that, running from his umbrella, spread themselves over the polished surface of the wood, prevented him from thinking of anything but his unpardonable stupidity. His native awkwardness became all the worse at this and, utterly unable to proffer any but the most confused excuses, he fled from the office of his chief leaving the latter in a high state of irritation.

He was replaced by some one else at the first opportunity, on the pretext that the direction of important affairs could no longer be left in the hands of a man of such notorious incapacity.

It should be added that this man was more than ordinarily intelligent and that his successor was by no means his equal.

It is, therefore, absolutely necessary for those who are lacking in presence of mind to accustom themselves to a species of rehearsal before undertaking any really important step.

Does this imply that they must think of nothing but weighty affairs and neglect occasions for social meetings?

By no means. To those who are distrustful of themselves every occasion is a pretext for avoiding action.

They should, therefore, take pains to seek every possible opportunity of cultivating poise.

The entering of a theater; the walking into a drawing-room; the acknowledging of a woman's bow; every one of these things should be for them a subject of careful study, and if, when evening comes, the daily self-examination leaves them satisfied with themselves, it will be a cause of much encouragement to them.

If, on the other hand, they have received a rebuff

due to their lack of poise, they should carefully examine into the reasons for this, in order to guard against such an occurrence in the future.

A good preparatory exercise is to choose those of our friends whose homes are unpretentious and who have few callers.

Let us make up our minds to pay them a visit, which, in view of the quietude of its associations, is not likely to awaken in us any grave emotions.

To carry this off well we should make all our preparations in advance.

One should say to oneself: "I will enter like this," while rehearsing one's entrance, so as not to be caught napping at the outset.

One should go on to plan one's opening remarks, an easy enough matter since one will be speaking to people one knows very well.

One should then decide as to the length of one's call.

One makes up one's mind, for instance, to get up and say good-by at the end of a quarter of an hour.

One should foresee the rejoinder of one's host, whether sincere or merely polite, which will urge one to prolong one's visit, and for this purpose should have ready a plausible excuse, such as work to do or a business engagement, and one should prepare beforehand the phrase explaining this.

Finally, one should study to make one's good-bys gracefully.

It might be as well, while we are at it, to prepare a subject of conversation.

Generally speaking, the events of the day form the topic of discussion on such visits, whose good-will does not always prevent a certain amount of boredom.

It will be, then, an easy matter to prepare a few remarks on the happenings of the day, on the plays that are running, or on the salient occurrences of the week.

It should be added that these remarks should express opinions of such a nature as not to wound anybody's feelings.

The man who seeks the conquest of poise will not expose himself to the risk of being involved in a discussion in which he will be compelled either to remain silent or to make an exhibition of himself.

To do this would be to strike a serious blow at his resolution to persevere.

The one idea of the aspirant to poise should be above all things never to risk a failure.

Such a check will rarely be a partial one. It will have a marked effect on his proposed plan of educating his will-power by again giving rise to that confusion which is always lurking in the background of the thoughts of the timid and which is, moreover, the source of all their ills.

Another wise precaution consists in foreseeing objections and in preparing such answers as will enable one to refute them.

Eloquence is one of the most useful achievements of poise; it is also the gift that best aids one to acquire it.

It is, therefore, indispensable to train oneself to speak in a refined and correct manner.

The man who is sure of his oratorical powers will never be at a loss. He will find conviction growing while he seeks to create it.

We spoke in the preceding chapter of the mechanical exercises necessary to make speaking an easy matter.

We must not forget, however, that before one can speak one has to think.

Words will spring of themselves to our lips the moment we have a definite conception of the idea they serve to present. As a proof of this contention one has only to cite the case of those persons who, while ordinarily experiencing great difficulty in expressing themselves, become suddenly clear, persuasive, and even eloquent when it comes to discussing a subject in which they are deeply interested.

The study of the art of speaking will become, then, for people of timidity, over and above the mechanical exercises that we have prescribed in a former chapter, a profound analysis of the subject on which they are likely to be called on to express themselves.

One should strive to describe things in short sentences as elegantly phrased as possible.

When the idea we wish to convey seems to be expressed in a confused fashion, one should not hesitate to seek for a change of phraseology that will make it more concise and clear.

But above all—above all, we must pull ourselves up short and begin over again if any tendency to stammer, to hesitate, or to become confused, begins to manifest itself.

Just as soon as one feels more at one's ease one can seek to put in practice all these special studies.

Nothing is quite so disconcerting as the idea of stammering or stopping short.

For this reason it is imperative that one should begin all over again the moment such an accident occurs.

This is what prevents timid people from accomplishing anything. From the moment of the first failure they become panic-stricken and can no longer go on speaking connectedly.

Those who would acquire poise must act quite otherwise.

Instead of avoiding occasions of speaking in public, they should seek for them. But first of all they must make some trials on audiences who are in sympathy with them.

They should experiment on their own families and should never fail to enlarge on their theme. If need be, they can prepare the matter for a short address or a friendly argument.

If they find themselves stammering or panic-stricken, they must strive to recall the phrase that caused the trouble and endeavor to repeat it very emphatically without stuttering.

For the rest, it is always a dangerous thing to talk too fast. Words that are pronounced more slowly are always much better articulated, and in speaking leisurely one is more likely to avoid the embarrassment in talking that attacks those whose education in the direction of the acquiring of poise is not yet complete.

One of the most important exercises in the search for poise consists in accustoming oneself to speak slowly and very distinctly.

If one stammers in the least degree, especially if this fault is due to nervousness, one should begin again at the word which caused the trouble, pronouncing each syllable slowly and distinctly. Then one should incorporate it in one or two sentences and should not cease to utter it until one can enunciate it clearly and without any trouble.

In order to combine theory with practice, one should seek opportunities for entering public assemblies, striving to do so without awkwardness.

One should choose the time when the audience is not yet fully arrived, since, unless one is very sure of oneself, it is a risky matter to appear on the scene when the house is full, or the guests for the most part assembled. By this means one is much more likely to be able to emerge victorious from the ordeal of the stares of the curious.

The man endowed with poise enters a gathering politely yet indifferently, ordering his manner not to suit the particular occasion but as a matter of instinct. He will go naturally to those whom he happens to know, will shake hands with them, and will say to each one the thing that he ought to say.

If a mother he will ask news of her children. He will offer congratulations to the man who has just been publicly honored. Presence of mind will not desert him for a moment; he will commit no blunders. He will avoid the necessity of meeting a former friend with whom he has fallen out and will pass him without speaking. He will not talk of deformities to a man who is deformed. In a word, his poise, while leaving him free to exercise all his faculties, will give him the opportunity to remember a thousand details, the performance as well as the omission of which will create much sympathetic feeling toward him among the people whom he meets.

The man who does not yet possess poise, will be wise if he follows the recommendations we have made, that is by preparing his speeches to be made on entering. In those cases where he is not absolutely sure of the relationship of people or of the condition of health of the person to whom he is speaking, he had better avoid these topics. Silence is not infrequently an indication of poise.

THE THOUGHT OF SUCCESS

But to emerge successfully from all these difficulties, one must believe that one can do it, banishing absolutely from one's mind the doubt, that, like leprosy, attacks the most well-made resolutions, transforming them into hurtful indecision.

The mere thought, *"I will succeed,"* is in itself a condition of success. The man who pronounces these words with absolute belief implies this sentence: "I will succeed because I will succeed and because I am determined to employ every legitimate means to that end!"

Avoid also all grieving or melancholy over past failures, or, if you must be occupied with them, let it be without mingling bitterness with your regrets.

Say to yourself: "It is true. I failed in that undertaking. But from this moment I propose to think of it merely to remind myself of the reasons why I failed.

"I wish to analyze them sincerely, while recognizing where I was in the wrong, so that under similar circumstances I can avoid the repetition of the same mistakes."

Fools and knaves are the only people who complain of fate.

The words "I have no luck" should be erased altogether from the vocabulary of the man who proposes to acquire poise.

It is the excuse in which weaklings and cowards indulge.

Timid people are always complaining of the injustice of fate, without stopping to think that they have themselves been the direct causes of their own failures.

The violet has often been quoted—and very improperly—as an example of shrinking modesty which it would be well to imitate.

It does not in the least trouble the phrase-makers and the followers of the ideas that they have spread broadcast through the world that the violet which hides timidly behind its sheltering leaves nearly always dies unnoticed, and that it is in most cases anemic and faded in color. The type that wins the admiration of the world is that, which, disengaging itself from its leafy shield, springs up with a bound above its green foliage just as men of poise rise triumphantly above the accidents and the petty details which bury the timid under their heavy fronds.

If one were minded to carry out the comparison properly, it is far more exact to liken the timid to these degenerate flowers, which are indebted to the shade in which they hide for their puny and abortive appearance.

The timid have then no sort of excuse for complaining of their ill-luck.

To begin with, it is to their own defects solely that their obscurity is due.

Furthermore, by ceaselessly complaining, they gradually become absorbed by these ideas of ill-fortune, which grow to be their accomplices in their detestation of effort and suggest to them the thought of attempting nothing on the absurd pretext that nothing they do can succeed.

One must add here—and this is extremely important—that in acting in this way they always manage to provoke the hostile forces that are dormant in everything and that array themselves the more readily against such people because of their lack of the resolution to combat them and the energy to overcome them.

This is the reason why people who are gifted with poise find themselves better qualified than others to succeed.

Their faith is so beautiful and so convincing that it compels conviction in others and seems to be able to dominate events.

It is by no means an illusion to believe in the worth of this confidence. People to whom it is given become of the most wonderful help to others, their faith aiding and sustaining that of those who have resolved to make an effort.

However strong the soul of man may be, it is nevertheless subject to hours of discouragement, to moments of despair, in which some comfort and sympathy are needed.

The man of resolution will recover from his failures the more easily the more certain he is that he has created in those about him an atmosphere of friendliness which will not allow his defeats to be made public.

As mists are dispelled at the approach of the sun, the agony of doubt will disappear in the genial warmth of the encouragement and the confidence that his poise and self-reliance have built up in those around him, and a sure faith will be given to him, the certain and faithful guide to the road that leads onward to success.

CHAPTER V

THE SUPREME ACHIEVEMENT

One must be most careful not to credit oneself with the possession of poise while one is unable to encounter reverses without loss of serenity.

Every setback of this sort must be judged without bias and the proper measures must be taken to prevent its recurrence.

Every exuberant gesture, as well as every constrained and abortive movement, must be the object of redoubled attention.

This is the stumbling-block that brings so many timid people to grief. They imagine that they have achieved the conquest of poise, while they are really only deceiving themselves by the idea that they are giving a good illustration of it. They become the victims of a peculiar type of delusion akin to that of the cowards who deliberately invite danger while trembling in every limb.

The very fear of being considered cowards causes them to plunge into it blindly without taking the trouble to reflect. They always overshoot the mark, exposing themselves quite uselessly and achieving a result that is entirely valueless to themselves or any one else.

The man who is really master of himself will avoid

such foolish undertakings, retaining his powers for those that are likely to bear fruit, whatever the quality of the success may be.

It is an act of folly to deny the possibility of success because one is discouraged at the very first obstacle.

The greatest triumphs are never achieved without a struggle. The man who obtains them does so only by virtue of the experience gained by repeated efforts, none of which bore for him the fruit he desired.

The better is merely a step along the road to the best.

Perfection is, therefore, the result of many half successes.

If one could hope to arrive at one stride at one's desired goal one's efforts would be of no value, and mediocrity would very soon become the sole characteristic of those who were possessed by this idea. The man who has had the wit to acquire poise will guard himself carefully from falling into the error of the timid, who, haunted by an unappeased longing for perfection, lose their courage at the first attempt.

Does this imply that idealism must be banished from the thoughts of the man of resolution?

Not at all, if by the word ideal one understands what it actually means.

A false meaning has been given to this word which has warped it from its original sense.

The ideal is not, as many people seem to think, an impossible dream indulged in only by poets, and that has no active basis of reality.

Lazy people abuse this word, which to their minds allows them to indulge without shame in idle dreams that foster their indolence.

The timid drape it about themselves like a curtain, behind which they take refuge and in whose shadow they conceal themselves, thinking by so doing to keep the vanity which obsesses them from being wounded.

Devotees of false ideals clothe them too often with the tinsel of fond illusion, under which guise they make a pretense of worshiping them.

The true ideal, that which every man can carry in his heart, is something much more tangible and matter of fact.

For one it is worldly success.

For another renown and glory.

For men of action it is the end for which they strive.

The ideal which each man should cultivate and strive after need by no means be a narrow aim.

It is an aspiration of which the loftiness is in no way affected by the lowliness of the means employed to realize it.

This word has too often been misused and exaggerated in the effort to distort it from its philosophical meaning.

In every walk of life, no matter how humble, it is possible to follow an ideal.

It is not an aim, to speak exactly, but still less is it a dream. It is an aspiration toward something better that subordinates all our acts to this one dominant desire.

Every realization tends to the development of the ideal, which is increased in beauty by each partial attainment.

We have just said that the ideal of some men is the acquisition of a fortune. It might be supposed, therefore, that such people, once they have become rich, will abandon their aspirations for something more.

The man who has this idea is very much in the wrong.

The state of being permanently wealthy is one that opens new horizons, hitherto closed. The doing of good, charity, the desire to better the condition of those who still have to struggle, these will constitute a higher and a no less attractive ideal.

This does not take into consideration the instinct, innate in every heart—and that the genius of the

111

race has made a part of every one of us—the desire of progressing.

It is this desire that forms the ideal of fathers of families, building up the futures of their children, in whom they see not only their immediate successors, but those who are to continue their race, which they wish to be a strong and virile one, in obedience to the eternal desire for perpetuating themselves that haunts the hearts of men.

It is quite evident that each gain has no need of being complete to bear fruit. The thing to do is to multiply it, to make something more of it, and to take it home to ourselves, in order to achieve the ultimate result that is termed success.

The man of resolution appreciates this fact perfectly, rejoicing in every victory and taking each defeat as a means for gaining experience that he will be able to use to his advantage when the occasion arises.

The man of timidity, on the other hand, haunted by this desire for perfection, cut off by his very aloofness from all chance of learning the lesson of events, will be so thoroughly discouraged at the first check, that he will draw back from any similar experience, preferring to take refuge in puerile grumbling against the contrariety of things in general.

This attitude of mind can not outlast a few minutes of sensible reflection.

We wish to convey by the use of this term the idea of a process of thought quite free from those vague dreams which are the sure indications of feebleness, reveries in which things appear to us in a guise which is by no means that which they really possess.

The main characteristic of this state of mind is to exaggerate one's disappointments while ignoring one's moments of happiness.

It approximates very closely to the old fable of the crumpled rose-leaf breaking the rest of the sybarite on his couch of silk.

He has no thought of taking satisfaction or pleasure in the luxury that surrounds him. He does not congratulate himself on his wealth, nor on the comforts he possesses and that he values so highly. He thinks of nothing but the little crumpled petal which causes him imaginary distress, and all his faculties are absorbed by this petty detail.

The man of resolve will pay no attention to such trifles as this. They will touch him not at all unless they assume the role of the grain of sand in the working-parts of a machine, which prevents it from running. He is wise enough to be able to estimate a situation sensibly, taking account of the drawbacks but at the same time realizing all the advantages that accrue from it.

At these advantages he will be pleased and will seek to get the maximum of good out of each one of them. If he thinks of the disadvantages at all, it will be merely in order to find a way to diminish them and to rob them of their power to harm him.

Such are the benefits of reflection and of concentration which, when practiced in a rational manner, will do more than anything else to help one to the attainment of poise.

Weak indulgence toward one's own failings will be rejected by the strong. To know oneself thoroughly is a good way to improve oneself, and the knowledge that one is not mistaken as to one's actual merits is of considerable help in acquiring poise.

It is for this reason that the habit of daily self-examination, that we recommended in the preceding chapter, develops, in the man who submits himself to it, faculties of judgment so keen that it is an easy matter for him to become his own educator in the path to betterment.

One great disadvantage of lack of proper concentration is that it gives to the subject one is anxious to study an importance greater than it really has.

Passion is too often an accompaniment of this form of reflection, emotions are aroused, and the nerves become active factors in distorting the real meanings and value of the things we are considering.

The remedy in this case is a very simple one. An effort of will, will readily banish the subject which is causing us too profound emotion by the simple process of turning the thoughts to some subject that will cause us no such disturbances.

Later on, when the emotions of the moment have passed, one can return to the former train of thought, forcing oneself to examine it with calmness.

Some amount of practice will be needed to acquire this mastery of one's thoughts, the parent of poise, which is nothing more than courage based on solid reason.

It may happen that the desire to follow a line of thought that causes us excessive emotion may lead to the inroad of a horde of secondary ideas, which press one on the other without any perceptible continuity, carrying with them neither conviction nor illumination.

Reveries of this sort are dangerous enemies of poise. They lead one nowhere, and create in us habits which are not controlled by reason or common sense.

If such thoughts should assail us, the sole means of avoiding injury from them is to repulse them instantly, the moment one becomes conscious of them, and to banish the chaos of scattered fancies by devoting one's whole mind to a single dominant thought that should be associated with the determination to obtain the mastery over oneself.

We have already suggested to the timid the advantage of foreseeing the objections that are likely to be made to what they may say. The mere fact that they have already formulated a mental answer will be a great assistance to the making of a successful retort.

To avoid still further risks of being confronted by a contradiction that may put them at a loss they will do well to adopt the following plan.

Let them put themselves in the place of the person to whom they plan to speak and then ask themselves if, under these circumstances, they will not find some objection to offer to the proposition concerned.

If they discover by this means that, in his place, they would be likely to find such and such difficulties, it must be with this fact in their minds that they devote themselves to the better preparation of their arguments or, if necessary, to modifying the force if not the content of the reasoning on which they rely to carry conviction.

These objections, as we have already advised, should be uttered aloud, so that we may the better perceive their logic, and also to allow of our repeating them a second time, the ability to accomplish which will be a great encouragement to us.

There is no reason, in fact, for believing that we can not repeat on the morrow, just as perfectly as we have expressed it today, a statement that we have made with clearness both of reasoning and of diction.

Contact with men and with affairs should be sought after by the aspirant for poise.

He will be the gainer by watching the destruction of his exaggerated ideas and his false conceptions, which have all arisen from solitary thought.

116

An essential point is to become accustomed to the necessity for action.

Far from avoiding this, one should seize every occasion to utilize it to one's advantage.

The determined student should even create opportunity for so doing, which, in forcing him to break down his reserve, will make it necessary for him to come to definite decisions and to carry them out.

Every chance to exhibit real and honest activity should be seized by him.

Between two decisions, equally favorable to him, of which one will leave him to his peaceful retirement and the other will involve active measures, he should not hesitate for a moment.

He will make choice of that which will compel him to exhibit physical activity.

It is, however, important that manifestation of purposeless energy should be rigidly repressed. They are always harmful to one's equilibrium and to the qualities needed for the attainment of poise.

One should never forget the well-known proverb:

"Speech is silver, but silence is golden."

Silence, in a vast number of instances, is the indisputable proof of the empire that one has over oneself.

To be able to keep quiet and to close one's lips until the moment when reflection has enabled us to discipline our too-violent emotions, is a quality that belongs only to those who have obtained the mastery over themselves.

The weak become excited, indulge in protests, and expend themselves in angry denunciations that use up the energy they should retain for active measures.

The man of resolution is most careful not to allow it to be known at what point he has been wounded. He keeps silence and reflects.

Resolves form within his mind and, when he at last is ready to speak, it is to utter some firm decision or to put forward arguments that are unanswerable.

To tell the truth, those who instantly and noisily voice their antagonisms, who, under the sting of a hurt to their vanity indulge in threats of violence, are actually dangerous.

Their accusations, dictated by anger and heightened by the sense of their own inferiority, are always characterized by impotence.

They make people smile, provoke perhaps a little pity, but never cause any fear.

They are like the toy guns of children, which have the air of being most deadly weapons, but which are constructed of such fragile materials that a vigorous blow will cause them to fall to pieces.

The self-control of the man of resolution in the face of insult and provocation is far more impressive than these idle threats.

His silence is ominous. It is a sort of mechanical calm which produces decisions from which all passion is excluded.

His answers, well thought out and adapted exactly to the circumstances of the case, impress one by their coldness and by their tone of finality. His words are always followed by deeds, and are the more weighty for the fact that one knows that they are merely preliminary to the actions that they foretell.

This is one of the marked advantages of those who possess poise, one of various methods of conquering and dominating the minds of others.

There are other strong points belonging to those who cultivate poise, which, judiciously employed, unite in giving them an incontestable superiority over the majority of the people they meet.

The man of poise will not be overly happy or too boisterous. Still less will he be taciturn. Moody people are nearly always those who are convinced of their own lack of ability and quite certain that the rest of the world is in a conspiracy to make them miserable.

They lack all pride and make no bones about admitting themselves to be defeated.

These, we must admit, are rather difficult conditions in which to effect anything worth while.

In "Timidity: How to Overcome It," M.B. Dangennes tells us that one day a party of men agreed to undertake a journey, the object of which was to attain a most wonderful country.

"There were a great many of them at the start, but only a few days had passed when their ranks became sensibly depleted.

"Certain members of the party, the timid ones, who were encumbered with a load of useless scruples, soon succumbed to the weight of their burdens.

"Others, the fearful ones, became panic-stricken at the difficulties they encountered in battling with the earlier stages of the journey.

"The modest, after several days' marching, fell to the rear, from fear of attracting too much attention, and were very soon lost sight of.

"The careless, wearied by their efforts, took to resting in the ditches along the road, and ate all their store of provisions for the journey without worrying at all about the time when they might be hungry.

"The braggarts and the boasters, after exhibiting a temporary enthusiasm, gave out at the first dangers encountered on the march.

"The curious, instead of striving to maintain the courage of those who walked at the head of the column, kept leading them into difficulties, in which many of the foremost were lost.

"The rash were greatly reduced in numbers by

their own foolhardiness.

"The final result was that only a handful of men, after many weary days and nights, reached the Eden that they had set out to attain.

"These men were disciples of energy, those to whom this virtue had given courage, ambition, the self-control and the self-mastery needed to vanquish and overcome the perils of the way; those who, by their cool and courageous bearing, had been able to impress on their companions, now become their disciples, the indomitable hardihood with which they were themselves filled."

We see in this fable how all the qualities of poise worked together for the accomplishment of the destined end.

First courage, which must not be confounded either with rashness or with effrontery.

Courage, the perfect manifestation of confidence in oneself.

This quality is at the bottom of all great enterprises, of which all the risks, however, have been carefully considered in advance.

The man of courage does not deceive himself as to the dangers of the deeds he has determined to perform. He accepts them bravely. He has foreseen them all, and he knows how to act in order to turn them to his own advantage.

The coolness characteristic of all men of poise gives them the power of estimating wisely how things are likely to turn out.

They do not fail to appreciate the importance of certain circumstances, to realize their bearing, and to admit the dangers to which they may give rise. Thus they are ready for the fray and are armed at all points for a well-considered defense.

Shame on the superficial people who close their eyes in order not to see the obstacles that their own lack of foresight has prevented them from anticipating.

Let us press back the timid; declare war on the boasters; show our contempt for the inveterately modest (who are only so to flatter their own vanity); express our hatred of the envious, who are always incapable; distrust the slothful; and arm ourselves with a justifiable pride, which, by imparting to us a sense of our merits, will enable us to acquire poise, true index of those who are legitimately sure of themselves and are conscious of their sterling worth.

But, above all, let us raise in our inmost hearts a temple to reason, the author of that quiet confidence that makes success a certainty.

This is the work of the man who has achieved the conquest of poise. It is the one particular evidence of this priceless quality.

Poise, by inspiring its possessor with a belief in his merits, that is productive of good resolutions, enables him to employ in relation to himself the fine art of absolutely sincere reasoning.

There are, as is well-known, many ways of looking at things.

Every thing has several sides and, in accordance with the angle at which we examine it, seems to us more or less favorable.

The superficial man only sees things, and only *wants* to see them, from the viewpoint of his own desires.

To the morose man all their contours appear distorted.

The optimist, on the contrary, carefully changes their outlines.

Only to the man who makes a practice of rational thinking comes a true vision of both the good and the bad that exist in everything.

This science of reasoning is the base of all deductive processes, that, in strengthening the judgment, aid in the formation of poise.

Without reason the scaffolding of the most splendid resolves falls to the ground.

Without reason we wander aimlessly in bypaths instead of following the broad highway.

Without reason, in short, we become guilty of injustice, not only toward others, but still more toward ourselves, since we can not form a correct estimate of our own characters.

It is reason which enables us to choose the happy

mean that leaves the country of fear to reach the goal of reserve, and follows it to the extreme limit of poise without ever encroaching on the territory of effrontery.

It is poise alone that enables us to communicate to others the qualities which we possess.

This has ever been the gift of men of genius, of those who could enforce their doctrines and impose them on others by the sheer strength of their attitude and the way in which they analyzed and reasoned out all their principles.

What conviction can he hope to carry to his hearers who is not himself persuaded of the truth of the theories he is presenting?

This is the condition of those timid people who give their advice in the same tone they would use to ask it.

For this reason they never become expert. They rarely ever taste of success and usually sink into a state of discontent and envy.

This last fault is nearly always indulged in by the timid, whom it soothes, not simply because of its maliciousness, but because envy seems to them to condone their own inertia by giving them an excuse for their lack of action.

For people of mediocre mentality to deny the intelligence of others is to bring them down into their own plane and saves them the effort of climbing to that of their superiors.

And since lack of sincerity toward themselves is always one of the faults of those who are wanting in poise, they can not help feeling a sentiment of jealousy toward those who have succeeded where they themselves have failed.

Instead of doing justice without bitterness to the superiority of others by a determination to imitate it, they take the simpler course of envying the good fortune of their neighbors and attribute it all to luck.

Whenever you hear any one expatiating on what he calls the luck of some one else, you may be sure that he is a person entirely deficient in those qualities which could attract what he calls luck, but what is really, in the majority of cases, merely the result of hard work based on a reasoned poise.

Here we may add that this quality is often the key to good fortune, since it permits the head of a family, who is possessed of it to establish about him sympathetic currents, based on the confidence that he inspires.

It is a matter of common knowledge how courage communicates itself from one to another.

The man who dreads the idea of doing something will attempt it without hesitation if he finds himself supported by some one who seems to have no doubt as to the happy outcome of the enterprise.

It is, therefore, most essential, in order to exercise a beneficent influence on his household, that the head of a family should be possessed of poise, which will awaken in them a sense of protection, while at the same time making them aware of a kindly authority.

It must not be inferred from this that every head of a family should pose as being infallible.

This would be a most foolish proceeding on his part. It would often happen that circumstances, by proving his predictions untrue, would destroy the faith in him that those in his household must possess.

It is only the presumptuous and the egotistical who pride themselves on their infallibility, as we have pointed out at length in preceding chapters.

The man of real poise will be more than careful not to pose as a prophet, still less as an autocrat.

He will study to establish about him an atmosphere of confidence suited to the development and the strengthening of the bonds which unite him to those of his household.

Nothing is more touching than the blind faith shown by some children toward their parents.

People of timidity will never arouse a feeling of this sort.

However real the affection of children may be for such parents, there will always be mingled with it a modicum of indulgent pity, caused by their distrust, if the parents happen to be people of timidity, of what seem to them mediocre abilities.

They will feel themselves more willingly attracted toward a stranger, if his attitude toward life appears to be one that may support and assist their weakness. Their affection for their parents will be in no way diminished, but they will cease to regard them as being vitally necessary to the harmony of their existence.

This lack of trust that timidity occasions can result in very serious misfortunes.

In driving a child who seeks for some firm guidance to appeal to others than his natural protectors, there is always the risk of his following a method of education that is basically opposed to all the traditions of the family.

How many children are thrown in this way on the tender mercies of a teacher whose views of life, albeit perfectly honorable, are quite opposed to the plans of the parents.

Such people, instead of complaining of the conduct of the teacher and crying out about the leading astray of their child, would do better to question themselves and to ask their own hearts whether their children have ever found in them the protection that is being given them by others.

We do not want to overwork the old fable of the oak and the ivy. Nevertheless, it is to the point to remark that this plant attaches itself to none but the most solid trunks, disdaining the Weaker saplings that will bend beneath its weight and will, after a little while, force it to return to the ground instead of helping it to climb into the air.

The man endowed with poise plays in his own family the role of the oak which lends the strength of its trunk as an aid to weakness, covering with the shadow of its branches the feeble efforts that too hot a sun or too violent a storm might easily bring to nothing.

And if the storm should break it is the crest that it presents with pride to the fury of the elements that will keep it from being itself destroyed.

It must also be remembered that the instinct of the Ego flourishes in every one of us, often quite unconsciously, but always with sufficient force to make it certain that this ego will be developed in the direction in which it sees chances of support.

We are not speaking here of mere egoism, which is a species of acknowledgment of weakness that very young children are incapable of making to themselves, but which those who are older will try to avoid.

But there is no one, even among the most strong, who has not felt at some time in his life the joy of finding counsel, moral support, or protection, if only in the form of a hearty and energetic agreement with his ideas.

One can not wonder, therefore, that people of poise are able to draw to themselves sympathies and devotion of which the timid are entirely ignorant.

We should add that poise, in giving one ease, imparts to the slightest gesture a fittingness that constitutes a special grace, that one can not always define, but where appearance can never be mistaken.

It might be termed distinction.

People of poise, whether they be homely or handsome, insignificant or imposing, sickly or radiating health, all possess this enviable gift in a marked degree.

Distinction is the parent of victory.

It conquers, for those who possess it, the greater part of their adversaries, who lay down their arms without dreaming of offering battle.

Distinction impresses every one, both those who are deprived of it and those who are possessed of it.

It is the most direct means of influencing others in the direction one wishes them to take.

It is hardly necessary for us to restate here that there must be no harmful influence in all this, no abuse of power.

Distinction is only efficacious and only possesses its proper force when it is the outcome of the qualities we have been endeavoring to inculcate in this book.

False distinction, that which is based on effrontery, is like those mirages of the desert whose appearance troubles the traveler.

At first he rejoices at seeing before him a

countryside that seems like his hoped-for goal, but as he presses forward the picture fades away little by little and he perceives that he has been the victim of an empty dream. This is invariably what happens when what appears to be distinction is founded merely on bravado and bluff.

The credulous, who are at first deceived by the illusion, very soon arrive at the point where they perceive their error, and, with the dissipation of the mirage, comes the contempt of the person who has thus made them take him seriously. They do not find it an easy matter to forgive him for having made dupes of them and their anger increases with the hurt to their wounded pride.

Those people, on the other hand, who possess that distinction that comes from the qualities inherent in poise, are sure of being able to preserve it untarnished, because their influence will never be enfeebled by disappointments they may cause in others.

If they are ever conquered for a moment, it is never because of weakness or lack of character.

Their defeat can never in any case be considered as decisive. Their energy will cause them to face the battle anew, armed by the very defeats of the past, and rendered invincible by their cool determination.

The mere habit of fighting tempers their souls and makes them strong, while the recollection of past reverses makes them more wary and more keen to take advantage of the lessons to be learned from events.

Thus they will not be slow in exacting that revenge from fate which will renew the confidence of all their friends.

They are a power, and under this title they receive the homage of all. Their existence is held to be a vital thing by all those who would stay their own weaknesses on their strength.

Their assistance may not always be effective, but it has the air of being so, and those who are afraid of failure are always anxious to have near at hand a force on which they can rely to keep them from defeat.

Every one who has helped to teach a child to walk has noticed that when its mother remains beside it and holds it up by the imaginary support of her hand, it steps out with confidence.

If she should go several paces ahead, the child, left to itself, and overcome by the fear caused by the withdrawal of her protection, which he really does not need, hesitates, stumbles, and presently falls down.

Men who are endowed with poise are not only appreciated by the weak of spirit, they are also esteemed and valued by those who possess qualities similar to their own. Such people are glad to meet a fortitude that approximates to theirs.

They are infinitely better fitted than others to escape the pitfalls with which the journey of life is strewn. If, in spite of everything, misfortune should attack them, they will meet it so bravely and will combat it with weapons of such unusual temper that it will hasten to beat a retreat in order to knock at the door of some timid soul, who will yield to it without a struggle and will allow it to take possession of him without a murmur.

www.ingramcontent.com/pod-product-compliance
Lightning Source LLC
Chambersburg PA
CBHW031515040426

42445CB00009B/242